Desert Sanctuary

DESERT SANCTUARY

Hank Messick
WITH A FOREWORD BY
Steve Allen

Come ye yourselves apart into a desert place, and rest awhile.
                                    Mark 6:31

University *of* New Mexico Press
Albuquerque

© 1987, The University of New Mexico Press
All rights reserved.
FIRST EDITION

Library of Congress Cataloging-in-Publication Data
Messick, Hank.
Desert sanctuary.
1. Arizona—Description and travel—1981–
2. Arizona—Social life and customs.   3. Messick,
Hank.   4. Retirement—Arizona.   I. Title.
F815.M37   1987   917.91'09154   87-10824
ISBN 0-8263-0996-8

Designed by Whitehead & Whitehead

To
Jeanne Williams
with thanks

Contents

Preface ix
Foreword xi
Bob's Bird 1
The Inspector 5
Water and Witches 10
Light 15
Home on the Range 19
Fireflies 24
The Wind 29
Rattlesnakes 33
Roses 38
The Nature of Barrel Cactus 43
Old Cat 48
Dreams 53
Ants 58
Rats 62
A Game of Inches 67
Progress 72
The Mad Bull 76
Mule Deer and Jackass Rabbits 81
On Bootlegger Saddle 86
Barriers 91
Snow 96
Rain 101

Old Things   106
Skeleton Canyon   111
Fear   116
Snakes Indoors   120
Tears   125
Moonlight Musings   130

Preface

I FIRST SPENT time in Arizona in the Sixties when I went there on the trail of the old Cleveland Syndicate. Working under a Ford Foundation grant to the Southern Police Institute of the University of Louisville, I studied the activities of such characters as "Gameboy" Miller, troubleshooter for the Syndicate, and "Butts" Lowe, a man with a ring in his nose.

Among other things, I inspected the Grace Ranch on the outskirts of Tucson. Owned officially by Peter Licavoli of Detroit, it had been for years a hideout for wanted criminals and a port of entry for illegal aliens, mostly Mafia members. Thanks to Police Chief Garmire, research went smoothly, and the day came when I felt I deserved a brief vacation before moving on to Las Vegas.

I drove out into the desert, south towards the border. Somewhere down there I parked my rented car and walked among the giant saguaros. Instantly, I fell in love with the desert and vowed that I would someday make it home. Would that I could have done so immediately while I had the health to fully enjoy the challenge; but I had work to do, books to write, battles to fight.

Two decades passed before I was free to consummate my dream. My sons preceded me, going to college at Northern Arizona University. Flagstaff was too cold, however, and my wife and I opted for the southeastern corner of the state where tall mountains rise above desert sands and physical conditions are not far from what they were when Coronado came through on his way to Cibola. No Apaches however.

The book that follows relates my adventures. It also describes a search for perspective, for meaning and purpose as time begins to run out. After all, one cannot divide his life into sections, each independent of the other. The past we bring with us.

While this is largely a personal chronicle, I would be amiss if I did not acknowledge once again my debt to my wife. Although slowed by arthritis, she has continued to be my loyal partner in all things possible. Together we found sanctuary in the desert.

HANK MESSICK

Foreword

WE AMERICANS often don't know who our heroes are. Oh, we hear of their names if the media publicizes their activities—we know about gifted athletes, courageous astronauts, brave soldiers—but societies often have to wait for the verdict of history to properly identify heroes. The situation is even worse at present in that, left to our own devices, we often wrap the mantle of the hero around the shoulders of rock singers, film actors or even successful criminals, while men and women doing truly important work in society, often against depressing or dangerous odds, go unheralded.

Some of our unrecognized heroes have devoted a great part of their lives to combatting crime and corruption. Hank Messick is one of those. In a purely rational and moral society—which is to say in a society that has never existed—those who are criminal and corrupt would be despised and those who exposed their evildoings would merit a special respect. In a society such as our own, however, one that is itself in large part criminal and avaricious, the modern follower of Diogenes is, at least by many, viewed as a boat-rocker, a trouble-maker, and a spoilsport. Witness the fate, for example, of F.B.I. agent Joseph Yablonsky in the corrupt community of Las Vegas. For exposing corruption he was subjected to very little praise and much abuse. Witness too, the fate of Hank Messick, who has written books about organized crime that ought to be in the personal library of every American citizen. Modern readers surprised to discover, from Kitty Kelley's biography of Frank Sinatra, that there is a close and long-standing connection between the entertainment industry and organized crime would not have been so startled had they been familiar with Messick's *The Silent Syndicate, Syndicate In The Sun, Syndicate Wife, Syndicate Abroad, Lansky, Private Lives of Public Enemies, Beauties and the Beasts,* among other well-documented reports by the same author.

The present reader will perhaps get Messick's overall achievement in clearer focus if he realizes that the writing and publishing of such revelations actually places the author's life at risk, not to mention the more subtle discouragements and disadvantages to which the virtuous are subject in a corrupt world.

But Hank Messick is more than a crime reporter, as was demonstrated by his *King's Mountain,* a history of the Blue Ridge Mountain men of the Revolutionary War. He is also an able analyst of inefficiency in high places, as he proved with his 1973 biography of J. Edgar Hoover (David McKay) in which he revealed that for a remarkably long time Hoover was not even aware of the existence of the Mafia, something on which millions of American citizens would have been happy to enlighten him.

Surprisingly, Messick works new ground in *Desert Sanctuary,* a charming, partly autobiographical and philosophical account of his life in the Arizona-New Mexico desert country. In his crime books Messick kept his own character in low profile, leaving the reader to construct a hazy image of an investigative crime reporter, almost like a character in a Dashiel Hammett or Raymond Chandler novel. But what emerges in the present work is a much more recognizably human figure, a new settler from the east, though not a big-city man. (His family background was North Carolina.) One interested in the beauty and grandeur of the still wild country of the southwest, its birds, snakes, rodents, coyotes, its cactus, rocks, backhills, rain-gullies, abandoned mines, and fellow residents.

As a former Arizonian I found Messick's evocations of the desert's scenery accurate and sensitive. He makes you feel the heat, the quietude, the serenity, and awe-inspiring timelessness of this particular corner of planet earth, and yet he does not view the milieu from some grand, impersonal, philosophical perspective. The close shots are in focus, too. The people, the animal creatures, the history all come alive in Messick's account, the writing as smooth and natural as one would expect from a former professor of English at Colorado A & M.

Although Messick's primary motivation in moving to Arizona was retirement he has by no means settled down to lick his wounds and rest on his laurels. He is still a foe of corruption, hypocrisy, and ignorance. As a student of history he is aware, for example, that Wyatt Earp, a Tombstone gambler, was a lawless gunman, a criminal. "Perhaps it isn't surprising," he observes, "that a people with a short and not too noble history have turned the facts around and turned Earp into a hero. . . . the town lives today on the legend, and tourists from all parts of the country come to walk the streets of "The Town Too Tough To Die" and go away believing in truth, justice, and the American Way. The sheriff who really cleaned up Cochise county, slight, soft-spoken John Slaughter, is almost forgotten. A true hero was Slaughter."

The true heros, as I've said, not only often aren't recognized in their own time, they can't even count on vindication by posterity.

Reading *Desert Sanctuary* helps us to appreciate the courage, wisdom, and sharp reportorial eye of Hank Messick.

STEVE ALLEN

Bob's Bird

A CALL FROM NBC News about a bird story was, to say the least, unexpected. I'm not a birder. When anyone out here in the southeastern corner of Arizona asks what I am, or was, I reply that I'm a retired people-watcher. Back when network news departments and newspaper reporters called routinely for information about gangsters, that's what they called me. Others had less friendly, more biased titles to bestow.

Portal, at the eastern gateway to the Chiricahua Mountains and my home, is largely populated by retired biology professors and their wives. There's also a floating cadre of active scientists in Cave Creek Canyon where the American Museum of Natural History has its Southwestern Research Station. Anything that creeps or crawls or soars gets attention, but birds are most popular.

Birders abound, but not one had seen a flame-colored tanager here or anywhere else in this country until Bob Morse spotted one in South Fork. A quiet, intense man with snowy hair, Morse quickly announced his find on the birder hot line. Within hours the invasion began as thousands came to see the tiny stranger. Inevitably, the Tucson press sent out photographers and on their heels came the television crews. Apparently someone mentioned my presence in the valley to the NBC crowd, for the caller said he needed to talk to me.

"Why?" I asked in sincere uncomprehension.

"I want to find out why you people come here to the ends of the earth."

The ends of the earth? Hardly. We are a bit inaccessible with our rugged mountains and paucity of good roads. That's why the Apaches under Cochise and Geronimo held out here for so long. Skeleton Canyon is just across the valley. High desert it is, but the Tucson International Airport is only three hours away.

"I didn't come here to look at birds," I told the caller.

He chuckled. "More birders I don't need," he said. "I want to, you know, balance the story. Birds and people, red canyon walls, and roaring white water."

Young and eager, he sounded. I once knew a TV reporter like that in Louisville. He eventually became a city judge in Chicago. Anyway, I told this one to come on out to "Treinta" if he wished, and he promised to call again when he was actually on his way. He still had some birders who wanted to talk to a camera to take care of.

I went out to the garden extension to dig postholes. The ground in rainless early spring was compacted, as hard as the rocks beneath the surface. My veteran posthole digger wasn't up to the challenge. The cutting edge soon became as jagged as the long reach of Portal Peak that loomed above me to the west. I kept digging until one of the handles broke. My shoulders ached. When you get a little older your muscles lose resiliency, or something. Now the problem was to find a new handle. There might be one in Douglas, some sixty miles away. If not there, then Sierra Vista, a hundred miles. Things in the West tend to be spread out, but it really didn't matter since plenty of other things required a pioneer's attention. The postholes would wait.

Late in the afternoon I went up the outside stairs to the deck of our solar home and settled down to look east across the San Simon Valley to the Peloncillos. The name means Little Bald Heads, so I've been told, and between some of the heads one can see the blue mountains of the Continental Divide. A purplish haze hung over the valley, making New Mexico look like the enchanted land it calls itself. The state line runs up the middle of the valley, but out there in a green sea of mesquite no one is exactly sure where. I'm pretty certain I'm on the Arizona side—the taxes are higher in this land of rugged individuals.

So the lad from the world I left behind wanted to know why I had left? That's what it amounted to, and it wasn't a simple question. Too complex for the few seconds the producer would allow. Once I was interviewed for three hours as part of a special on crime. When the show aired I had been cut to twenty seconds at the very end. By then anyone watching had gone to sleep.

A buzzard just back from his winter sojourn in Mexico, circled far up in the dark blue sky. He moved effortlessly, riding the air currents, looking for food. Was the true purpose of life a hunt for food, for protection against heat and cold? It often seemed that way in the desert. Only man seeks for more than he needs to survive, whether it be material goods on earth or treasure in heaven.

In my small way I had been different. Coming out of the Blue Ridge Mountains of North Carolina, I rejected the Scotch-Irish philosophy that accepted poverty and looked to heaven for reward. Not wealth, but a chance to improve the present became my goal and a job as a muckraking reporter seemed a way to achieve it. Over the years that followed I raised plenty of hell, had my guts almost scared out of me, got indicted, assaulted, and libeled. I could count the scalps of sheriffs, police chiefs, politicians and gangsters, but in the end I knew I had changed very little. Lincoln said you can fool some of the people all of the time and that, I found, was usually enough to permit continuing corruption.

Could I tell the man from NBC that I came to the high desert because I was all burned out? Since it had the virtue of brevity, it might suffice, but it would be only a part of the truth. As a reporter I had always sought the truth, be it balanced or not. Perhaps I should resume my personal journal; I always thought better with my fingers on a typewriter. Patterns emerged, facts fell into place, and the obscure became logical.

My musing was abruptly interrupted by the panting of a large dog. I glanced around in alarm. Nothing. Then I remembered and looked upward. A raven, blacker than the buzzard but smaller, had flown directly above me on his way to a nest at the base of the mountain. The panting sound had been caused by his wings. At low elevations flying was hard work. The first time I heard the sound I questioned several birders but none had ever heard the beating of a raven's wing.

In the room below, the telephone rang shrilly. Faye answered on the second ring. The conversation was short so I lifted my heavy body from the chair and went down from the deck.

"The NBC man can't make it," my wife said. "Too many birders. He apologized sweetly and I told him you wouldn't mind a bit."

I didn't mind.

In time, a two-minute segment appeared on the Today Show. Devoted entirely to the little bird and its finder, it said nothing about the ends of the earth or why people went there. Armed with binoculars and camera, Bob Morse was shown fording Cave Creek on stepping stones and explaining that birdwatching is not only a fun hobby but good exercise as well.

And I began writing again.

The Inspector

WHAT WAS the roadrunner called before there were roads?

I began asking the question early on. When the walls of our poured-concrete home arose where before there had been only mesquite, a roadrunner appeared to walk carefully along the top. The contractor, a man of no small imagination—especially when he was explaining away delays—called the bird "the Inspector" and assured me his presence meant good luck. (The contractor eventually fell off the roof and broke his back.) It wasn't until a forty-foot wall of glass was installed, however, that the roadrunner became a frequent visitor. He would run madly along the ground in front of the glass, his neck and tail extended, his crest erect and bristling, and turn abruptly to peck savagely at his reflection. Another dash, another savage attack, on and on for an hour or more. For variety, or perhaps because the floor was smoother, he would move up to the deck where smaller clerestory windows offered similar opportunities. Many a morning after the house was finished I awoke to the sound of conflict and usually thought of the quote about life being a walking shadow full of sound and fury signifying nothing. Or something like that.

There was no pattern to the Inspector's visit. Days would pass without him and he arrived at any time of day that struck his fancy. Every other animal or bird I saw in the wild seemed engaged in a ceaseless quest for food—was the roadrunner the only one that took time to play?

The full-grown Inspector measures two-feet from bill to tail. His legs are long, about four inches, and each has four toes with two of them facing backward. One back toe is reversible, an aid to perching. His long beak is slightly curved downward, and he clacks the lower against the upper to make a sound like a machine gun. A member of the cuckoo family, he has yet another sound for mating: a long, drawn out "coooooo." He puts his head between his legs and slowly, slowly, lifts it as if with great effort. The cooing sound emerges. When he finishes he wags his tail up and down as if to pump in new energy, and then repeats the process. The sound is easily imitated, and often I disconcerted the Inspector by doing so. Always he looked startled, but upon spotting the source he would flip his tail in disgust. Any fool could see we weren't compatible.

Once I happened to be on the deck when the bird arrived. He retreated as I walked slowly toward him, then he hopped up on the parapet. Within three feet of him, I held my left hand straight out and twitched my fingers. As his eyes swiveled, I lunged with my right. All I caught were two tail feathers as he took off in a long glide to the ground. The feathers were greenish black with white tips.

Brown and white color his upper body and gray is below. His crest is black and ragged. The area immediately below it is lovely—black, blue bronze, and green—and sets off the bright, mischievous eyes with their flecks of yellow. In winter on a cold morning he changes, looking much like a round, fluffy ball. He pulls in his head and lifts coarse whitish down around his folded feathers. He stands where the first light of the sun strikes and as he warms he slowly changes to his more familiar shape.

Some months after the house was completed I provided the Inspector with a new game by building a six-foot high fence of chicken-wire around my newly replanted orchard. The Inspector was quickly on the job. He flew over the fence and began a routine mad dash, stopping to poke his head violently through the holes in the wire mesh. It was great fun apparently, and when he had enough he flew out. But things weren't so simple for his mate.

At least I assume it was his mate. She was smaller, less colorful, and hadn't been around very long. Somehow she got into the orchard and couldn't get out. She, too, raced along the fence, poking her head through the wire, but there was an air of desperation about it. By the time I happened upon her she was nearly exhausted. I caught her in a corner. Neck and head were bloody, and her heart beat fast, but her toes wrapped around my fingers and held tightly. Not knowing what else to do I took her to the kitchen sink and let water run on her head. Part of it got into her mouth and she seemed to choke. Some experts say the roadrunner doesn't drink, but when I built a fountain in my yard I found otherwise. He or she approaches cautiously, lowers the head and jumps around to make sure nothing is sneaking up behind. After several such feints, the drinking begins. The bird can't swallow, but tilts his head up and lets the water drain down, which is perhaps why the one I had captured choked. It was then I found she had eyelashes and something that looked like mascara on them. So she had to be female.

When the bird began to struggle slightly, I put a strip of raw meat in her beak and set her outside. For a full minute she was motionless, then, abruptly, she flew up into a mesquite tree, the meat still dangling from her beak. I saw her around for several weeks and then she was gone. Which raises a somewhat sinister question.

Back when the house was still under construction, I spotted the Inspector coming out from his nesting area with something heavy hanging from his beak. When he dropped it and hurried away, I investigated and found a dead roadrunner. It was just slightly smaller than the Inspector. I could see no marks of violence. Was it a discarded mate that the Inspector had terminated with extreme prejudice and carried from the nuptial nest? Was it an older son who had tried to take over the homestead? Or was it the Inspector's aged mother?

There was no way to know so I shoveled the body into a javelina hole, long since abandoned, and covered it up. Giving things a "decent burial" is really rather silly out here. Ranchers leave cows hit by cars where they fall along the roadside. Eventually, they dry up.

For a few weeks after the mate I rescued disappeared, the Inspector seemed subdued. He's getting old like the rest of us, I told my wife. But one morning there was the old sound and fury at the window and he was obviously in good spirits again. In time I saw him with a mate. In fact, I saw them in the act of mating. When it was over, the Inspector strutted around just like a triumphant rooster. And, eventually, two young birds appeared. They had a great time eating grasshoppers in my garden and gave every indication of being a happy family, but then I found the body of one of the youngsters and my old doubts revived. Does the lovable roadrunner kill his mate when he's through with her? Does he kill his children when they hang around the home nest too long? The birders I asked seem to know little about the private lives of roadrunners, apparently considering them too common for study.

The reputation of the roadrunner as a killer is well established. He's supposed to be able to take on rattlesnakes and swallow them whole after pecking them to death. Perhaps. But not even the Inspector could swallow the huge rattlers that inhabit the high desert around here, and I doubt he would try.

There's a lot of other misinformation about the bird. Some writers tell you they will race cars and trains. Perhaps in the days of wagon trains they ran along the road, but in modern times they race across it. Maybe they sense they can't outrun an automobile, but they sure as hell can get across in front of it. On only two occasions have I seen them start and, realizing they weren't going to make it, turn back just in time. They are fast, but whether they can outrun a racehorse, as some experts say, I don't know.

I'm not completely without answers, however. I can answer my question: "What was a roadrunner called before there were roads?"

I didn't get my answer from birders. They told me the Mexicans call him "paisano," meaning "countryman." So I did some research. John G. Bourke mentioned the bird in his classic account of the war against the Apaches, *On the Border with Crook*. Writing in 1891, Bourke told of "the swift-walking, long-tailed roadrunner, the 'paisano' or 'chapparal cock' . . ."

But there were roads of sorts in those days. I needed earlier testimony. I found it in an 1859 article by an army surgeon, Dr. B. D. Irwin. He said the bird was known to the Mexicans as "paisano" and to the Anglos as "the prairie pheasant."

So there.

Dr. Irwin, incidentally, also wrote that "the small feet" of Mexican girls were "bewitchingly pretty." He was twenty-nine at the time.

Water and Witches

ONCE THE decision is made, for whatever reason, to move west and seek sanctuary in the desert, two major questions arise:

Where can you find land offering beauty and solitude at a price you can afford?

And will there be water on or under it?

I've read several books purporting to be about life in the desert, but in the end it appears the writer was living in the suburbs of Tucson or Phoenix. He could hear coyotes occasionally, and perhaps see a deer, but he also had the advantages of water, sewer, and electrical systems. That's not pioneering exactly, and, in any case, unless you're prepared to spend a fortune for an acre of land it really isn't practical anymore.

The Chiricahuas in general and Cave Creek Canyon in particular are known in scientific circles worldwide for their natural beauty and animal life, but until recently the scientists managed to keep it all a secret. Many retired here, continuing their studies at their leisure, and doing their best to maintain a closed society. The break came when a large ranching enterprise decided to subdivide its thousands of acres and sell them in forty-acre parcels for from $250 to $500 an acre. We happened to be in Arizona at the time, saw a small ad in a Tucson newspaper, drove down in a rented car, spent two hours looking at land, made a down payment on a parcel we liked, and went home to spend the winter wondering if we had lost our minds. The following spring we returned to stay a week and went away delighted.

I don't recommend anyone follow that example. Arizona has had its land frauds and will, I'm confident, have more. But the vital question is water. The state is literally mining its water, pumping up more than nature returns to support a growing population. Agriculture takes a fantastic amount. Here in the San Simon Valley cotton is a big crop. Apples, pears, and peaches are grown. The soil will produce anything—if it is irrigated. Cities such as Tucson would have no future were it not for the Central Arizona Project which is supposed to bring water from the Colorado River over the mountains sometime in the next decade at a cost of billions of dollars to United States taxpayers. Better, in my opinion, to find a remote area where land is relatively cheap and the water table is comfortably high.

Which brings me to water witches.

Despite what a skeptical science may say about dowsers and their divining rods, the folks in rural Arizona believe in them. Only they are called water witches, regardless of their sex. People here talk about a New York attorney who bought a lot of land across the valley in New Mexico, built an imposing house with a stone wall around it, and failed repeatedly to find water. Finally, as an act of desperation, he paid a locally famous water witch $100 to tell the drillers where to try next. At 307 feet they struck it wet.

"I was so delighted," said the attorney, "I almost kissed the old bitch, er, witch."

Instead, he gave her a bonus.

Perhaps the most unique witch in the valley is Hal

Mortensen, a weather-beaten, rawhide tough rancher in Price Canyon. His divining rod is a plain old metal coathanger, cut in the middle to form a Y. Grasping an end of the Y in each hand, he extends the stem horizontally, belt high. He walks in circles until the end of the hanger dips sharply toward the ground. Below, is water.

But that's not the best of it. The dips continue and Mortensen counts them. When the wire stops moving he knows exactly how many feet down it is to the water. Two hundred dips, two hundred feet. He can't explain why or how a wire coathanger should have such power, and he admits a few failures over the years, but nine of ten times he proves out correct.

No one had ever drilled on the mountain slope where we elected to build, and there were predictions we'd have to go a thousand feet or more. Our well-driller was more confident; he, after all, had the "power" and used his own personal divining rod on the theory that "if it gives us an edge, why not use it?"

Ernie's instruments were two brass rods two feet long, with a six inch bend at right angles for handles. He taught me how to use them. Grasp the handles and extend the rods straight out and parallel as you begin your search. When the rods move to the right or left, you are approaching water. When they cross each other you've found it.

The brass rods won't tell you how deep you must drill. Ernie had tried the clotheshanger method without results. Apparently the body chemistry, or electricity, or something, of the witch determines which works best. Some people—my son, for example—simply do not have the gift, if gift it is. Later, I got myself a pair of brass rods and conducted additional tests, happy to be able to attest that the movement of the rods was spontaneous. I located an old septic tank for a retired professor and I found water on top of Rattlesnake Ridge for a young carpenter who had just paid for a dry hole at the bottom of the ridge. Turned out, however, that there wasn't enough water at my location so he returned to the dry hole and went down several hundred additional feet where he found a little more. My most obvious success came when I stepped on a rock in the middle of Cave Creek and held one rod above my head. It began revolving like a helicopter blade.

To each his own.

Meanwhile back to the rocky mountainside where the jackrabbits and mule deer play. One afternoon while waiting for the boss driller to show, Faye and I counted twenty-one deer coming out of our property to cross the road into the wilderness of the desert floor. We found nature thrilling, but man's inability to keep appointments and schedules was frustrating. Time was running out. I was overdue back in Florida to complete the intimidation of a federal bankruptcy judge in another state who allegedly was aiding some crooked lawyers rob a dead man's Florida estate. We had four days left and we desperately hoped to find water before leaving.

Ernie, a stolid, heavyset man of German descent, promised he'd do the best he could but no one knew what was down there until he drilled. The rig was old, using thickened mud to carry up the crushed rocks and soil. It broke down often. Newer rigs using compressed air could do the job in hours instead of days but they were expensive and, as Ernie's boss saw it, unnecessary in an area where he had no competition.

That's a point to remember when settling in a remote area. It applies to more than well-drillers.

The first two days things went as expected. There were a lot of boulders of all sizes down there, a fact I later personally confirmed. But on the third day the drill hit gravel. It was easy to bore through, but when Ernie pulled up the drill to insert a pipe, he discovered the hole had caved in.

Progress became slower and slower. On the day we had to go, we delayed until 1 P.M. for, abruptly, the drill had fallen three feet and was spinning around uselessly. We discussed an alternate site, and left with a heavy heart but with confidence in our new friend. Ernie Rothpletz would not drill 500 feet just to run up the bill; of that we felt sure. But, of course, he might have to go deeper to find the water his magic rods had promised. And at thirteen dollars a foot, depth was money.

That evening we called from Florida. Ernie's voice sounded sleepy and far away.

"Guess you're a pretty good water witch," he said. "We found water an hour after you left."

They had used compressed air, somehow, to get the goop flowing out of the hole again and discovered the drill had reached a deep cavern just 135 feet down.

"You've got a river down there," said Ernie. "All the water you'll ever need."

We went to bed happy.

Light

ARIZONA HIGHWAYS is a wonderful magazine, catching the beauty and infinite variety of scenery as well as providing glances backward into a colorful past. Its staff, however, seems to lack a sense of humor.

One of its cover pictures inspired me to write a letter to the editor. The picture was designed to illustrate the lead story about ghost towns, and it showed a wall of rough wood against which was a work table. A hand-cranked telephone was fastened to the wall. There were some faded tobacco cans, a leather pouch out of which spilled gold nuggets, and a revolver. In the center of the table was an oil lamp. Cobwebs covered everything, including the lamp. Obviously the place had been long abandoned.

Yet the oil lamp was burning brightly, its glow keeping at bay the surrounding darkness and making the nuggets glitter.

Amazing, I decided, so I wrote to the editor to inquire what manner of fuel the lamp contained to keep it burning so many, many years. I thought my tongue was clearly visible in my cheek when I suggested the fuel might well solve the energy problem.

As a boy growing up in the Blue Ridge, I learned a lot about oil lamps, and I carried many a gallon jug of kerosene home to fill them. Kerosene only cost fourteen cents a gallon in those days, but some folks in Happy Valley thought the Messicks extravagant for using two lamps to read by. Indeed, some thought we were nuts to be reading so much in the first place.

When my father pioneered the first successful rural electrification cooperative in North Carolina, we threw the oil lamps away, never dreaming that within a few years antique dealers would be combing the hills for them. Life changed drastically for us and for millions of others in rural America, the Southwest included.

On occasion when involved in a discussion of things in general with a native Arizonian of conservative persuasion, I delight in asking how long he and his neighbors would have waited for electric power had they been forced to depend on private utilities. Portal, I'm convinced, would be waiting another hundred years had not an REA cooperative out of New Mexico provided service. Its lines penetrate canyons and isolated valleys, going wherever there is someone to use it. Apparently, however, the co-op has learned some lessons, for it will not build until a well has been drilled and water found.

So it was that we could not get the power line extended down the road from Portal until Ernie found water. And then we had to pay half of the construction. Since I could see the line from our house site, I didn't think it would amount to much. In the days of my youth when I helped survey REA lines, we cut across country on the theory that a straight line is the cheapest. Sometimes they used oxen to pull in the poles, so rough was the territory, but they got them there. In Arizona, however, the co-op insisted on marching down the highway, and making a right-angle turn up the hill to the house site. It made the line more expensive, but what good is an underground river unless it can be brought to the surface? Moreover, the

Contractor informed me that he had to pump plenty of water in order to mix his concrete on the site. By then, of course, I was back in Florida, and had to make arrangements by telephone to get the power line built, the pump and water lines installed, and a septic tank placed down hill from the house.

When the bills began coming in, I suspected I was being robbed. Most suspicious was the charge for putting underground the service wires from the transformer pole to the house. Blandly, the Contractor explained that the boss of the work crew had a fight with his crew and ended up demanding they not only put two feet of fine sand in the trench to cushion the wires but that they also place the wires in a special plastic pipe.

It sounded strange to me then but a couple of years later when I needed to run an extension off the main line, I dug down and found the plastic pipe. This time, however, the work crew came without their boss and accepted sand as sufficient. It was one more proof to me that the wise home-builder will be on the scene to watch every step of the program. It isn't that Arizonians are crooks, you understand, but apparently some of them not only believe that Eastern folks are effete but also have too much money for their own good.

Not all new pioneers are willing to pay the costs of extending the power line. About two miles down the mesquite from us, a couple pulled in a trailer and began building their own house at their leisure. Instead of central station power, they installed solar panels and generated their own.

This is a fairly recent development in the West and credit for it should be given, in part, at least, to the marijuana growers of northern California. They are, and want to be isolated, and they don't want meter-readers coming around, so they began buying solar panels on such a scale that an industry to supply them developed and brought the price down. Tax credits helped as well. In fact, we seriously considered going that route and still hope to install a system in conjunction with the co-op. We would use the co-op's power on cloudy days.

If only the marijuana growers could get the price a little lower.

In any event, when we were ready to move into our new home we didn't have to depend upon oil lamps. And that brings me back to "Arizona Highways" and its long-burning lamp. In response to my letter, I soon got a note from the editor saying he had referred it to the photographer for reply. A few days passed and along came a letter from famed photographer Jerry D. Jacka. He wrote:

> *To answer your question, I used kerosene in the lamp . . . but that is not what provided the light for the photograph. I used a Norman 2000 studio strobe with one diffused light head. The diffused light was also covered with a yellow-orange filter to give the photograph the warm light effect. I positioned the light so it would appear the lamp was providing the light in the photograph.*
>
> *I hope this information is helpful to you.*

Well, it doesn't help solve the energy problem, that's for sure. And I still don't know why they wanted a lamp burning in a ghost town anyway.

But perhaps I just don't like oil lamps.

Home On The Range

So you've had a dream for years, a dream of a house uniquely yours in a setting of big sky, wide valleys, and surrounding mountains capped with snow. You're ready to retire and you're tired: weary of traffic jams, pollution, snow, and people en masse. Your children are grown and gone, preoccupied with building their own families, needing you no longer.

What to do?

Go west, old man, go west.

The Sun Belt includes Florida, of course, and I spent sixteen years there. It is lovely, warm, and wet. If you or your wife develop rheumatoid arthritis, you need a dry climate. Perhaps for that reason, Arizona ranks right behind Florida in the number of new residents. They come here to live out their last years and, having done so, go back to where they came from to be buried. At least according to a study, 17.1 per cent who die here in the Grand Canyon State are shipped elsewhere for burial. But that's incidental. Outside of Mexicans and Indians, it's hard to find an elderly native son in this state, which means, I think, that there's still plenty of room here.

There's also plenty of room in New Mexico and Texas, and living conditions are rather similar. One can find planned communities for retirees. Places like Green Valley south of Tucson have homes to fit upper middle-class budgets and beyond. They offer every service possible including social directors. The place is pleasant, friendly, and secure, but essentially it is an old folks home. If there's still some juice in your system, you won't like it.

A community more to my liking is Carefree, north of Tucson. Requirements are strict, stylewise and pricewise. Homes must merge naturally with the sand and rock environment and cost a minimum of a quarter million. Not exactly a pioneering way of life but ideal for tired executives who land on the private airstrip nearby. Apparently, they enjoy living near the intersection of Ho and Hum Streets.

Years of stress had given me hypertension on a dangerous level. My doctor said I needed peace and quiet and physical challenges to keep my once-tough body in better shape. My choice, then, was limited: I needed, as well as wanted, to play pioneer. No comfortable suburb of Tucson would do, no planned community of wealthy retirees, no product of another man's mind. By luck we stumbled on the Chiricahuas and Portal. When Ernie found water, our last obstacle was removed. Or so we thought.

Faye had been designing our retirement home for years so we didn't really need an architect. But where to find a contractor? While waiting on the well, we talked to the owners of new homes and came away depressed. One man said it had taken four years to get his house built. A succession of contractors from as far away as Tucson and local "Handy Andys" had taken turns, each working on the house when he had nothing closer to home or more urgent. On a hill high above Portal the same thing was happening. Martin and Kay Muma were waiting on a specialist in rammed earth homes to get on with their two-foot thick walls. Fortunately, Martin had an outlet for his frustrations. When things got too bad he retired to a rented apartment across the valley and continued his life-long study of bugs. Eventually, the Mumas had to sue their contractor, and find other people to finish the house.

A third house was under construction on the site of Galeyville, once a small mining town and headquarters for the rustlers who roamed Cochise County in the 1880s. Every splinter of wood had been salvaged by residents of Paradise, a community higher on East Turkey Creek. Brooks White bought 500 acres and after a year had only the foundation poured. His Tucson contractor had simply given up and walked away.

That was the problem—only when the construction industry in the urbanized areas was in trouble would contractors consent to build near Portal. Everything had to be hauled in: lumber, insulation, roofing, concrete, and windows. Locally, there was an abundance of rocks, but skilled masons capable of using them had to be imported from Mexico.

Only Alden Hayes, a rancher turned archaeologist "in order to eat," seemed to be making progress on an adobe house at the entrance to the canyon. The bricks of dried mud had been formed on the property thanks to an unusual deposit of clay. Assembling them into a large solar house was a concrete contractor from far across the county. Years before he had done some work in Portal and was happy to come back. Alden was away on a "dig," or something, when we went up to see his house and meet his man. The house was impressive with its south wall of glass and beehive fireplaces. Nor were we disappointed in the articulate contractor who showed us around and used the editorial "we" at every opportunity. He gave the impression of heading a large operation, reaching from El Paso to

San Diego. Tall, handsome, with a ready smile, he allowed that he would be happy to build us a home while he was "on the ground," so to speak.

We checked out the possibilities: a conventional ranch house of wood, a rammed-earth home, an adobe structure. All were expensive, none carried a completion date.

The Contractor, as we continued to call Hayes's man, was persistent. Faye liked his ideas, but I was turned off until he began talking of poured concrete. He'd never built one, of course, but he knew it would work. And, moreover, it would be fast. Why, with a bit of luck, he could have the shell finished in six weeks. Model it on Alden's house.

Faye brought out her house plans and in short order they adapted them. We would have a solar house complete with Trombe walls of glass, clerestory windows, and a concrete deck instead of a roof above half the house. Would it be strong enough? Why, sure; in fact he'd drive his tractor up on it to prove its strength.

"It would withstand an earthquake," he added solemnly, "and that's important in Arizona."

We agreed on a price for the shell—I intended to finish the interior myself—to be paid in installments as the work progressed. And then we shook hands on the deal. No contracts, no lawyers, no red tape; this was the Western Way, sir.

Of course, it was all subject to Ernie finding water, but that proved no problem. Back in Florida I began making repairs on our Peace River home preparatory to putting it up for sale. Faye flew to England to visit a sister. And the rains began.

A month passed and Contractor called. He was now free to begin work so how about some money?

"Sixty days?" I asked.

"With luck," he replied.

I wrote a check and put it in an envelope. Then I called the lodge in Portal where we had stayed before, and reserved the apartment for two months, beginning in ten days. I looked at the rain falling on the cypress-shrouded river and told myself that in Arizona, at least, it would be dry.

And the desert would be blooming.

Six months later the desert was white with snow. The Contractor was in the hospital with a broken back to match his broken promises, but the house was almost livable. I arranged to have tile laid and the plumbing connected in our absence, and we went back to Florida to sell the house and terminate our affairs. In the spring we drove back with our furniture, bucking headwinds and sandstorms. We moved in almost a year to the day that Ernie hit water.

Everyone congratulated us.

Fireflies

THOSE MONTHS in Arizona while the new home was built were somewhat similar to our honeymoon years in Colorado when all was fresh and strong and life was fun.

The necessity of keeping an eye on the Contractor restricted my roaming, but I had time to explore the canyons and hidden valleys around Portal. Once each week we went to Tucson where a doctor to whom Faye had been referred monitored the Gold Salts treatment for arthritis. Otherwise, my time was my own to answer any challenge that presented itself.

Adding to my contentment was the absence of newspapers and television. For the first time in my adult life I knew nothing of what was going on in the world and had no interest in becoming informed. Faye made friends with the women of the area, many of them former teachers, artists, and writers, so I had no qualms of conscience when leaving her alone. Moreover, much of my activity was concerned with making our new abode more interesting.

Early on, I collected rocks. Boulders is the better word. Curiously, they were often arranged above as well as below ground in veins as if ancient lava flows had conveyed them. I selected pretty ones and created semicircular driveways, parking areas, and paths to meander through a garden of cacti I planted. To supply colorful rocks for the large fireplace of native stone, I searched far afield. Dry creeks had lovely rocks but I was warned they might explode if heated. I learned of an abandoned marble quarry but could not find a block small enough to carry to the truck. I did discover a large chunk of crystal which fitted nicely just below the mantel.

It was all good exercise and even fun.

Eventually, when the west wall which contained no window, was erected, I decided to build a double carport there of pole and frame construction. It was then I found that wood in the desert is a scarce commodity. There are plenty of giant pines, maples, even cypress, high in the Chiricahuas, and the early settlers made great use of them. Since the mountains became part of the Coronado National Forest, logging has been severely restricted. When a railroad running down the valley was discontinued a few years back, the railroad ties disappeared overnight as residents grabbed them up. The same thing happened when the telephone line was put underground a year or two later.

My scouting around paid off, however, when I found there was still a telephone line running across the hills to the little community of Paradise on East Turkey Creek. Most of it was in the Forest which explains why it remained. Another reason was the terrain, all hills, steep and rocky. Yet I had snaked large chestnut trees off equally rough territory in my youth, and this figured to be no more difficult. That I was a little older didn't bother me. Physically, I felt young.

The first step was to get permission from the telephone cooperative to dismantle its line. No problem, except I was told I must also have the consent of the land owner. The Forest Service was cooperative as well, recognizing that in removing the lines I would be erasing a blot on the fair face of nature. Permission, however, was conditioned on my agreement to haul away the "entire" line: Poles, wires, insulators, and any other foreign objects.

Having nothing better to do, I accepted. Two of the poles were actually close to the road that wound its crooked way to Paradise. I cut them first. Making them fit on a shortbed truck wasn't easy, but I let them poke out to the right and drove, when possible, on the left side of the road. Then the real fun began.

I fashioned sort of a harness. Tying the ends of a twenty-foot strand of telephone wire to the large end of a pole. I made a loop and got inside of it. When I pulled, the wire cut into my belly so I found a short piece of wood and placed it between my flesh and the wire. That worked well. I loaded a shoulder pack with insulators, grasped my axe with my left hand and the chain saw with my right, stepped into my harness, and started down the mountain.

It wasn't easy but I enjoyed it.

Upon obtaining all the poles that seemed accessible, I turned to the problem of removing the wire. I didn't want it but had promised to take it. The strands were long, as much as 400 feet where the line had leaped from ridge to ridge. Individually, they pulled easily, and I was able to get the ends down to the road.

Faye was a bit shocked when I announced I was going to pull the wires home late at night. It sounded underhanded, even crooked, but I explained that there would be no traffic at that hour to get tangled in my wires. Son Hank came down from Flagstaff—where he was courting a girl and working on his second or third college degree—and agreed it would be an adventure.

Actually, there wasn't much to it. We fastened three or four wires to the trailer hitch of the old pickup, and drove slowly along the narrow, rocky road. The wires followed along peacefully, taking the curves and not getting tangled in bushes along the way. When we hit the paved road above Portal, however, we had fireworks. Friction caused sparks. It was beautiful; in the darkness they looked like a stream of dancing fireflies following us home.

Through sleeping Portal we went without incident, and two miles later were safely on our property where we dropped the wires in out-of-the-way places. Faye was so intrigued by Hank's account, she went along the next night and enjoyed it.

On subsequent nocturnal excursions we met a vehicle only once. It was on the paved road below Portal and I saw headlights in ample time to pull off the road and stop. He went by slowly and put no strain on my load when he crossed it. Ironically, that single individual who saw me pulling wires proved to be a telephone company employee. A year or two later we happened to be talking and I mentioned where and how I got the poles for my carport. He laughed.

"I saw somebody pulling wires one night, but it wasn't any of my business. I knew the wire wasn't any use anyway."

Hank went home and called his brother, an electrical engineer in Florida, to tell about all the fun I was having. Jon had attended Northern Arizona University too, and he was also having woman trouble. A little peace and quiet seemed in order, so he took a week of vacation and flew out. We managed one more wire run for his amusement, but then he decided he wanted to get above it all. A climb to the top of Silver Peak intrigued him upon discovering that only five or six hardy souls try it each year. Perhaps up there in the solitude, he could decide if he really wanted to marry the girl.

I had to accompany him, of course. No one climbs alone in the Chiricahuas—not if he has good sense. It was a strenuous six miles across the face of the mountain, switch-backing up to an abandoned lookout station 7,975 feet high. As we climbed the view across the San Simon Valley and far into New Mexico became entrancing and provided excuses to stop and rest. The silence was complete and as far as the eye could see peace pervaded.

Just as we made the final charge to the top, a helicopter came fluttering up, its motors making an obscene racket. It landed on a flat spot near the lookout tower, and a half-dozen men jumped out carrying chainsaws, hammers, and other tools. The chopper took off gracefully and dropped down into the valley to return with several sheets of plywood dangling from a cable.

The men explained they had come to repair the old lookout tower, just in case. They went to work, banging, sawing, and yelling, with the thin air magnifying the noise. Jon sat down on a rock, staring glumly eastward toward Florida and the girl who waited there. I tried to talk the helicopter pilot into flying us back down. No luck. The racket continued atop Silver Peak so we headed home. Going down was almost as bad as coming up, and we reached the car exhausted. I could still marvel, however, that I had walked—let alone climbed—twelve miles.

Jon went back to Florida with blistered feet and a private heart. When eventually we also went back to get our furniture and sell our Peace River house, we enjoyed a Christmas family reunion, complete with grandson. It was dampened, however, by memories such as the Christmas Eve in Fort Lauderdale when the managing editor of the Miami Herald called to warn me that a contract had been issued for my life. I sat with my back to the wall at Christmas dinner.

The new memories were better. Pulling four hundred feet of fireflies through Portal in the dead of night had been more fun.

The Wind

ALONG BYWAYS and highways of the Southwest one often finds sections of road marked with seemingly contradictory signs. One tells you that this is a flash flood area and another warns of sand storms.

It really isn't inconsistent. Most big sand storms come in March and April; the rainy season doesn't unofficially begin until July 4. There are exceptions. In Arizona one may have a devastating flood in late September, and the wind is liable to start blasting any time a winter storm drops too low as it sweeps across the Northwest. Sometimes storms slop over the Continental Divide from the east. "Back door" blows, they are called.

As noted we fought headwinds while driving our rented van through Texas. North of San Antonio on I-10, the wind slowed us to a crawl. It took all my strength to keep the gas pedal down and the high-profile vehicle in the road. Up ahead the sun was a hellish yellow blur, and as the gasoline gauge dropped toward empty we finally found a motel in Van Horn. I was utterly exhausted, but I had a heavy respect for what I dubbed "a yellow devil."

High winds hit the Portal area within a week of our arrival. They swept out of the southwest, blowing anything loose into New Mexico and throwing sand against our south-facing wall of glass. Night came and still the wind howled. Faye took her tired body to bed, but I stayed up to listen to the moans, shrieks, and whines of the wind. I'd never heard such a variety of sounds and, afterwhile, I realized I was nervous.

Wind, after all, is an elemental force, and its demanding screech stirs ancient memories and primitive fears as old as man: fears of gods and demons, of forces too powerful and mysterious to be comprehended. A helpless feeling is part of the emotional process. One can do nothing to stop the unleashed fury outside the walls. Hunker down and wait.

Later, I learned to put loud classical music, preferably Wagner, on the stereo and take two sleeping pills. Combined they seemed to neutralize the enemy without. On this first night, however, I walked the floor and searched for a reason to explain my unease. And, suddenly, I found it.

The Trombe wall, that forty-foot long expanse of glass on the south side, was moving with each gust. I put my hand against it and felt the surge, an inch or more. I turned on more lights, peered and probed. There were, dammit to hell, no braces fastening the glass to the intervals of inner concrete wall. The six-foot high glass wall was anchored at top and bottom and at its ends, but there was nothing to stop the center from moving like a live thing. How long could it stand the pressure and what was happening to the seal that allegedly made the double-glazed glass both air and water tight?

Well, there was nothing I could do about it at midnight in a wind so strong it almost knocked me down when I crept outside for a better look. So I went to bed and covered up my head. Next morning the wall was still in place and the wind had died. I drove to Alden Hayes' house, on which mine had been modeled. Yes, there were braces every eight feet along his wall, built in as part of the construction. And we had used the same man.

Rusty Boss, son of rancher friends down the valley, took a look and manufactured a set of wrought-iron braces which we placed at eight-foot intervals. And when next the wind blew hard I could detect not even a tremble of the glass, although I still cringed at the sound.

Fears over the safety of the Trombe wall were replaced the following year by worry over the metal roofs I had placed on various outbuildings I managed to construct: carport, pumphouse, and a bunkhouse for guests. The metal was heavy and well screwed down, but after the first big blow of the new season I went back and added more screws. They cost seven cents each and you can use a drill to put them in place.

Much later I built a double carport some distance apart from other buildings. One November afternoon the first "cut-off low" of the winter came roaring in and blew stoutly all night. At daybreak I inspected the new building and discovered the roof was lifting as much as a foot at the southwest corner. The wind, I was astonished to find, had unscrewed the nuts on the bolts that held the roof beams to the supporting poles and had pushed the bolts out of their holes.

Quick action saved my roof and left me more than a little in awe of my adversary.

In summer the wind takes the form of "Dust Devils," isolated little twisters that pick up dirt and carry it far and wide. From high on the side of a mountain one can look across a desert floor and count a dozen "devils" at a time. Strangely enough, they are often triggered by jackrabbits. Due to natural features of the ground, air in summer sometimes gets heated in spots out of equilibrium with the air around and above them. Air at ground level may be superheated to 150 degrees, while a few feet above it may be only 100 degrees. If a jackrabbit comes loping along, his movement can cause the superhot air to rise. This sucks up surrounding air and a spiral develops and becomes a Dust Devil. Sometimes they stay more or less stationary and sometimes they move at as much as forty miles per hour. Allegedly they've lifted kangaroo rats, whose mounds of tunnels are easily scooped, high into the air and deposited them unhurt but unhappy in the next county.

My experience with Dust Devils was not nearly so dramatic. I had just finished spreading dead leaves, gathered in the National Forest, on my garden preparatory to turning them over into the newly dug soil. Newly but not easily dug; the rocks I had taken from the garden I used to build a low wall 140-feet long to divert rain water from the house. Anyway, after all that work, along came a Dust Devil and in an instant all my mulch and much of my soil went spiraling up into the dark blue sky.

It was so ridiculous I had to laugh.

Rattlesnakes

Descending the shoulder of Portal Peak, I moved slowly, enjoying the long view across the valley and beyond, and cherishing the fact that home was in sight and only a mile away. It was early morning and I had been for a ramble. The slope was littered with small red rocks and the ground was the same color. There were several towering century plants in various stages of decay, and a few bushes of juniper and silver spruce, but the wind speeding across the ridge kept it relatively clear of vegetation.

The whirr of a rattlesnake's tail.

I jumped with a fear instilled in infancy back in the Blue Ridge where rattlers and copperheads were the chief source of worry for young mothers. When I toddled out of the house I wasn't warned of strange men or speeding cars, but rather of snakes.

There, ten feet ahead, stood the largest rattlesnake I've ever seen. Yes, stood. He was coiled in a tight circle, ring upon ring until his ugly triangular head was poised more than two feet from the ground. The tail was free at the bottom of the pile and was buzzing angrily. Yellowish diamond-like markings dominated, giving the appearance of human excrement. Shit, that is.

The head was in constant motion, back and forth, up

and down. Those movie heroes who shoot off the head of a rattler must be pretty good. I could've done it, maybe, if I'd had my shotgun.

It was a standoff. The rattler stood his ground, defending his territory. According to experts, the Western diamondback is the largest western rattler and the most dangerous snake in all North America. This character must've been the granddaddy of them all. I edged in, trying to get close enough to count the rattles, but the snake drew back his head. For all I knew he could strike the length of his body, so I retreated, picked up a rock, threw at the head, missed, tried again and hit the body, then picked up a larger rock with both hands and heaved it. Somehow the coil of snake dissolved as the rock approached and the body slithered aside as it landed. Granddaddy struck once at the small boulder, leaving a stain of venom or saliva I didn't investigate, and unhurriedly slipped away to the left.

Later, other people reported seeing a huge rattler in the same area, but, as far as I know, he is still as free as he should be.

With my early training, reinforced by some uncomfortable experiences later in life, it was something of a shock to come to Portal and meet men who believed the rattler should be protected. Bob Chew, a retired biology professor, informed me that when he saw a rattler on the road he'd stop and herd the creature off the blacktop to protect him from other motorists who might deliberately run over the snake to get his rattles.

Ranchers in the area who routinely kill every rattlesnake they encounter, found added evidence in this attitude that the "environmentalists" are "different." This hostility to snakes doesn't derive from personal fear, as does mine, but from economic reasons. The rancher seldom gets off his horse when working cattle so it is the horse that gets bitten when he chances upon a diamondback. And a good cow-pony is valuable. The newcomers to the area, "the environmentalists," persist in believing the proper way to treat a deadly snake is to trap him, somehow, and then transport him many miles away to an uninhabited area where he can live in peace.

As usual, I find myself in neither camp. If I meet a snake, or anything else in the wilderness, I'm happy to leave him or it alone. If, however, I find a rattler near my home, then he's going to die if I can manage it.

Killing a rattler isn't an easy task sometimes. I found one in October in the middle of my driveway about noon. As my pickup truck approached he coiled and struck at the big tire. I backed up to find I'd missed him, but apparently he decided it was mismatch and started for the mesquite. I quickly followed and ran over his full length, literally squashing his body from his skin. Yet the now white body continued to coil and strike blindly. Even after I cut off the head and hung the remains on a mesquite bush, the reflex action continued for more than an hour. It was ample proof to me that it's best not to get close to a rattler, dead or alive.

There is a third opinion on rattlesnakes in the area, however, and it holds that they are mighty good eating. I learned this one day when two Mexicans stopped by for water. Called "Wetbacks" because the main border crossing once was the Rio Grande, these illegal aliens had crossed a fence near Douglas and made their way up the valley on foot in search of work to feed their desperate families south of the border. Each carried a plastic water jug and a sort of knapsack out of which extended stiff white somethings-or-other about three feet long.

Somehow, we managed to communicate, and I discovered the white things were dried rattlesnakes. With a few snakes and plenty of water, they explained, they could walk a hundred miles through the mesquite. Rattlers were prized as food in Mexico, they added, and taste much better fresh than dried.

With plenty of hot chili peppers, no doubt.

I broke off a piece and chewed it carefully. It tasted like a dry stick. White teeth flashed and the younger of the two men rubbed his belly, indicating I knew not what. Assuming in any case that they probably needed something to supplement their diets, I gave them some bananas and four cans of potted meat. They refilled their water jugs, thanked me politely, and headed north into the mesquite. Talk about living off the country, these guys knew how to do it. I hoped they'd find a job soon—even ten dollars a day and "found," as the ranchers put it, would be better than dodging the Border Patrol and eating rattlesnakes.

In September the rattlesnake does his duty to perpetuate his species. Often he will take possession of a kangaroo rat mound with its series of tunnels. If the rat takes the situation philosophically, the two may co-exist; if he objects he's likely to be swallowed by the impatient snake. The young are born live. Poke a stick down the rat hole and the resulting buzzing sounds like a hive of bees.

Duty done, the snakes all disappear as cold weather approaches. They find a safe spot in a remote area and virtually hibernate. Rancher Roy Boss found himself sharing a cave with a den of rattlers one cold January day. He had taken shelter when overtaken by a downpour and was considering spending the night there until he spotted the snakes. They were awake, he said, and watching him but making no move. He was happy to leave them alone as well.

Occasionally, someone will set fire to a pile of brush under which a den of rattlers is concealed. A loud sizzling noise results and when the fire dies there's nothing left of the snakes. They are quite literally melted.

Beware of rattlers, but don't be afraid to go hiking in mid-summer. The snake isn't going to ambush you. Make enough noise and he'll challenge you. It is, after all, his territory. Heave a rock or two at him and he'll move to the safety of a mesquite or yucca bush. At home, a cat or two is helpful. They kill rats on which snakes feed, and they've been known to take on the snake himself. Or so some people say. I cut off a hunk of a rattler once and offered it to my old cat. She approached cautiously, sniffed, jumped backward three feet, and ran.

Roses

ST. VALENTINE'S DAY was approaching and I was in a quandary.

Where in a wide world of desert and mountain was I to find a dozen roses?

For more than thirty years the birthday of St. Valentine had carried a special significance for Faye and me and today, in a new home in a state still strange to us, it was more important than ever. The giving of roses was an act of love, of course, but also, in a peculiar, personal way, an act of defiance.

It began during my first newspaper job. After three years of teaching journalism to cowboys in Colorado, we returned to western North Carolina bringing with us a new addition, a year-old daughter. In my wisdom, I decided that to be a good teacher I needed newspaper experience. It's an old-fashioned idea today, of course, but it still makes sense to me. I'd mapped out a program and the semiweekly Waynesville "Mountaineer" was the first step.

Truly, it was an education. I covered everything from farm festivals to high school football games, and I learned what I was not supposed to cover. The editor and publisher was a frightened man and saw no evil. I, of course, saw plenty of it, bootleggers, cops with criminal records, and stores near the high school that sold liquor to kids on their lunch breaks. I slipped some of it into the paper and aroused the crusading spirit in a few newly returned veterans who were tired of the old way. The Editor was not impressed, however, and after several unfruitful discussions I gave notice. It was time to move onward and upward anyway.

Word of my impending departure didn't reach the police station in time apparently, for after lunch one day, I found a big, fat cop waiting for me in the parking lot. He grabbed my glasses from my face with one hand and swung with the other. I was in pretty good shape, however, and still had the reflexes of a boxer. I ducked, and only a heavy ring on his pinky scratched my head. He was pretty well tanked up—you could smell the moonshine—and I was curious. He kept swinging and cussing, and I learned he had decided on behalf of the cops to teach me not to stir up trouble.

The discussion carried across the street to the newspaper office where the staff had watched through the window. All but the Editor—he had locked himself in the men's room. The cop became impatient and started throwing more punches that I had no trouble ducking. Once when he lost his balance and fell across a desk, I warned him not to hurt himself. The women became hysterical and began laughing. Promising to get me later, the cop staggered out.

The word got around town fast. When quitting time arrived I found a dozen good citizens, some of them armed, waiting to escort me home. They formed quite a caravan. As we passed the police station they blew their horns. Home was a couple of miles away, and about half way there I realized it was St. Valentine's Day. I detoured a block out of the way to stop at a drugstore. The column of cars halted behind me while I went in and bought a large heart-shaped box of candy.

When we got home my protectors allowed me to go in alone, kiss my wife, and explain. Then a delegation entered and we had a party. It was fun for awhile, but I developed a splitting headache and a sense of futility. Much more happened later, of course, but the incident brought me and my wife closer. The following year in another city, we marked the occasion with roses. Faye was watching her diet and off candy. Becoming more special with each passing year, the tradition continued.

So here we were in the deserts of Arizona and it was important to prove to Faye that one thing, at least, had not changed.

But how?

I secretly called the florist's shop in Douglas to learn their rose supply was limited and they doubted a single petal would be left by February 13. So I parked myself near the Portal post office and began questioning men as they arrived to get their mail. Most were elderly, and seemed puzzled by my need. A couple, however, said they had heard of a rose farm over in Animas Valley.

A rose farm in the desert? It sounded a mite unlikely, but it was the only lead I had.

By good luck, the Chiricahua Art Group met in Paradise on the day before St. Valentine's which meant Faye would be absent for several hours. As soon as she departed, I headed across the valley for Animas. It's just east of the Peloncillos and has a large high school but not much else. The Postmistress confirmed there was a rose farm or something up the valley near Cotton City. I followed her directions and headed north past endless fields of plucked cotton. This valley was also wide and largely empty, but eventually I reached a church that had been a brick schoolhouse, and turned east toward the Continental Divide. Up ahead a mass of buildings materialized into a complex of huge greenhouses. Rose farm indeed!

I got directions from two young Mexicans working in one of the greenhouses, and finally found the "Cool Room." There more Mexicans were working, trimming leaves off long-stemmed roses, and wrapping them in newspaper. One youth got on the phone and an Anglo appeared. I explained my wants and he said a dozen roses would cost me fifteen bucks. Ordinarily, they didn't cost so much but St. Valentine's Day brought the greatest demand of the year.

On the radio that morning I had heard that a dozen roses was bringing eighty-five dollars in New York City.

The man opened a heavy door and led me into the "Cold Room." There thousands of roses in a variety of colors were waiting to be moved to refrigerated vans and hauled east to El Paso and cities along the way.

"Tell you what," said the Boss. "There's twenty-five in each bunch. Give me twenty bucks and we won't have to split one."

I selected yellow roses and when they were completely wrapped in newspaper and placed in a plastic bucket of water, the man followed me out to the car.

"How is it possible?" I asked, gesturing at the dozen greenhouses, each a hundred yards long with steam pipes along each row of roses.

The man grinned. "Thermal springs," he said. "There's boiling hot water just 130 feet down. We pump it up and let it circulate through the greenhouses. Engineers tell us we can use steam to generate electricity, but, so far, there's not much demand for it."

All this, just a valley away.

I got home before Faye, hid the flowers in a cool place, and next morning filled every vase in the house with long-stemmed roses.

Faye was, to put it mildly, astonished.

A couple of years later there was an ironic sequel. I received a call from a reporter on the Waynesville *Mountaineer*. He was also, he admitted, the nephew of my old Editor who was semiretired. The lad was well spoken and had done a good job of running me down. He had a request. The fiftieth anniversary of the paper was coming up and, naturally, they planned a special edition. Would I write an article for it, telling of my experiences and observation of the paper and the town? They would pay for it.

"They wouldn't print it," I told him.

"Why not? You're a well known writer and some people still remember you around here."

He sounded like a nice kid so I didn't laugh.

"Ask your uncle," I suggested. "If you can get a promise to publish I'll write it for nothing."

He never called back.

The Nature Of Barrel Cactus

A STORMY DAY in November, damp, raw, cold. The hill, the valley floor, are as gray as the clouds which creep slowly down Portal Peak, reaching, searching. Faye has gone to a meeting of her quilting club and I have no urgent tasks. A sad day, somehow, yet I can't pretend it is unique. The sun will return tomorrow or next week, yet that knowledge brings no pleasure.

Preparations for moving west kept me busy for a year, and the months since we arrived have been filled with the work required to turn a forest of mesquite into a home. There's been little time to think about the past, to grapple with personal problems, and today I discover they didn't remain in Florida when I left. Nor will they vanish, I suppose, tomorrow or next year, so how could one wish to live forever?

Time defeated me, I guess. A friend once wrote a magazine article in which he noted that I had won enough victories to know I couldn't win the war. True enough, I suspect, but so long as I was able to fight it didn't matter so much. More changed than my health. The cycle of reform, the one that began with Robert Kennedy, ended. People stopped asking what they could do for their country and greed became fashionable. Crusading went out of style. Nixon lost his battle but won his war.

I snorted in disgust. Was I calling myself a victim of social change? Were all my efforts wasted? Had I been a fool to try? Couldn't I have found a better use for my dedication? And why was I so damned dedicated in the first place?

To hell with it. I put on a ragged windbreaker and picked up a mattock. A couple of weeks earlier while on a ramble I spotted what appeared to be a giant barrel cactus on a south-facing spur of the mountain. Already I had collected two smaller specimens and planted them near the front door. Why not investigate instead of vegetate? I needed exercise.

To reach the hill through the mesquite was no problem. With the leaves gone and what little ground cover existed dead with the first frost, I could thread my way across the rocks and sand without difficulty. But there were several deep washes dug by the torrents of summer. Getting a wheelbarrow across them wouldn't be easy, I told myself, and shrugged. Answers weren't coming this day. Let it lay.

The hill was steep and the clouds sent down streamers to greet me. I aimed at the giant stalk of a century plant, and then went left to a lone creosote bush. Just above it was the cactus, the largest one of its kind I had yet seen growing wild. The damned thing came up to my waist. I doubted if I could get my arms around it. A prize indeed.

Today I know a little more about barrel cacti. They have been much romanticized as the source of lifegiving moisture to cowboys stranded in the desert. One can cut off the top—if he has a machete or sword—and squeeze fluid from the pulpy mass within. While round, the body has pleats and some writers maintain that in periods of prolonged rain the cactus will absorb so much water the pleats will flatten out. Not so. I experimented with two smaller specimens, one of which I watered daily and the other I ignored. The two remained identical in size and shape.

The important thing to remember about barrel cacti is they are covered with pin-cushion spikes. Since the thorns turn inward at right angles it is possible to carry a cactus if you handle it carefully. If you don't use caution you can lacerate your hands and clothing.

There was no chance I could carry the monster I had found on this dismal day, it was far too large. Yet my mood was one of black depression and I wasn't going to walk away from this problem. I took the mattock, swinging it at a 45-degree angle. Sparks flew as steel hit rock. Down on my belly, I moved dirt with my hands, stabbing my wrists as I did so. The shallow roots of the cactus had enveloped a large stone. No surprise—I had encountered it before. Some experts say that stones absorb water and the roots of the cactus excrete an acid which penetrates the rocks and draws out the moisture they contain. Stability is also achieved by using rocks as anchors, for unlike such desert plants as mesquite, a cactus has no deep root system, making them relatively easy to dig up.

Since I couldn't dislodge the rock without injuring the roots, I dug a wider circle around my giant and eventually used the mattock to push it over. It fell, still clutching the round limestone, and I freed the remaining roots.

Now what?

I couldn't lift the damned thing, that I knew. At a guess, I estimated its weight at 300 pounds. If I could get it to the bottom of the hill, perhaps I could get it into a wheelbarrow and roll it to some place I could reach by truck.

A squall of fine rain wet my face. I lifted my hand to wipe my eyes and noticed that blood from punctures had made red mud of the dirt on my fingers. What a day! Using my mattock, I positioned the cactus so it would have an unimpeded roll, and I shoved it with my foot. It rolled like a log, bouncing a couple of times, but heading straight and coming to a stop in a fairly shallow gully at the bottom of the hill. When I examined it for damage, the rock was still clutched to its dirty bottom.

I hiked home, loaded a light-weight wheelbarrow into the pickup, and drove as close to the hill as I could reach. Then I half-carried the wheelbarrow to the gully where the giant cactus lay.

It didn't work. I couldn't get the damned thing into the barrow. I tilted the barrow to one side, got part of the cactus in it, and broke the handle when I tried to pull it upright. To hell with it. The clouds covered the valley floor now and it was becoming cold although I was wet with perspiration, dirt, and blood.

Leaving the cactus where it lay, I dragged the broken wheelbarrow back to the truck and went home. A hot shower didn't improve my feelings, and I didn't sleep well that night. In the hour before dawn I resolved to go back to the gully, sit the cactus on its end, and pile some dirt around its roots. Maybe it would live.

Morning came in sunshine and, over coffee, I abruptly decided I wouldn't quit so easily. I borrowed a larger, heavy-duty wheelbarrow and took it in the truck back to the battlefield. This time I managed to roll the cactus into the barrow and set it upright. Down the gully I pushed it, to a juncture with another, more shallow wash. By great tugging I pulled my load up the side to level ground. Stopping to rest often, but feeling a growing sense of satisfaction, I zigzagged my way through the mesquite until I came, inevitably, to the deepest arroyo of them all. There was no way around—this was one dry river I had to cross.

Getting the cactus to the bottom of the huge gully was simple; I let it roll down. And then I got to the bottom with it and began rolling it up the other side. My gloves and the pin-cushion nature of the thorns protected my hands, but, God, it was heavy. Inch by inch I rolled the monster until, at the last, I lay flat against the side of the arroyo, my arms extended above my head, my feet braced against the bottom. I was just long enough to push it over the top.

I sat a long time before climbing out of the hole and pulling up the wheelbarrow to put my prize back in. There was a proper way to do it but an awful effort was necessary. Across the sand we went until the truck was reached. I had brought along a heavy plank to form a ramp and, rather to my surprise, it worked. Slowly I drove home, afraid a jar might topple the wheelbarrow and spill the cactus. Once there, I dug a deep hole and slid the cactus, still clutching its rock, into it.

A small victory, but it made me feel better. The morbid thoughts of yesterday came to mind. What the hell! We go where the engine takes us and do what we're designed to do. To wish things might have been otherwise is a foolish game, and in the end it matters not a damn. Who said all questions require answers?

The big cactus seemed happy at first, producing a crown of yellow fruit. Then, despite my efforts, it began to shrink and shrivel. Only later did I discover the barrel cactus leans to the south and is called "the compass cactus" for that reason. I'd placed it on a north-facing incline. The poor devil strangled itself trying to twist around.

Once again I had won a battle and lost a war by trying to make something act contrary to its nature.

Old Cat

In 1968 I lost a daughter and gained a cat. Marda went off to college, a sweet and eager girl. At Christmas her younger brothers gave her a kitten, but already it was apparent she had put away childish things. Left behind when vacation ended, the cat somehow became my responsibility.

Almost before I knew it, my daughter was married and I was a grandfather. A second child followed quickly—youth of that decade believed in Love and Nature. My son-in-law was a hairy adolescent who was not unhappy to quit school and support his family as an apprentice carpenter. When eventually he began to grow up, my daughter took the children and went back to college. Soon she found a lonely graduate student willing to marry her and adopt her children. Ultimately, history repeated itself but at least there were no more kids.

Meanwhile, I had a cat, a rather nondescript creature, brownish in color with spots of black. In Fort Lauderdale where she grew up, she was content to stay home and run the place. We permitted her to experience the joys of motherhood only once before taking her to the vet. Otherwise, my wife and I became, in effect, her servants, providing food, opening doors, and playing with her when, very infrequently, she was in the mood. To be candid, she tolerated Faye and turned to me for affection.

Writing was my business and I had a large, book-lined study in which to do it. Cat kept me company. Entering noiselessly, she would leap smoothly to my desk and curl up in a half-empty box of typing paper. I typed, she slept. Togetherness!

On many a cool evening she accompanied me on a walk along New River. As I looked in vain for a bundle of cash abandoned by a doper—other people found them—Cat stared with interest at the world of boat people, staying five feet behind my heels. We took her to the beach and she was not impressed. Ignoring the tide, she found shade under a palm tree and waited for our foolishness to end. When occasionally we went away overnight, a neighbor supplied food and water and Cat would be waiting in the driveway when we returned.

The years went by, the boys went off to college, my wife became a real-estate broker, and one book followed another. Cat was a constant factor, never changing, content with life as she knew it. We bought land on Peace River in DeSoto County and eventually built a house upon it. The river rolled by a front deck which was shaped like the prow of a ship, and hundreds of trees shut out roads and people. As a weekend retreat it was just about perfect, but when we took Cat to see it she took exception to the strangeness and sat on the roof the entire weekend. Thereafter when she saw me loading the car for a trip to the S.S. (Stationary Ship) Treetops, she disappeared into her own secret place. Adventure, she did not want.

Ultimately, we decided to go west. Selling our Fort Lauderdale home was the first step. Moving temporarily to Treetops was the second. Cat had no recourse but to go along.

Some weeks were required, but gradually Cat adjusted

to country life and found pleasure hiding in the palmetto thickets until she tangled one day with a wild creature and emerged bloody and battered. After that, she stayed on the deck from which vantage point she could watch the fish leap, the alligators sun themselves on the opposite bank, and the canoes go by.

It was a lovely place with its Spanish moss and ancient oaks, and I enjoyed fishing for bass and catfish. Yet it was also humid and the time came to move on. When we drove west to oversee the construction of our solar home, we took Old Cat. She hated to travel and at motels along the way she hid each night in the box springs. I'd have to turn the bed upright to shake her out. Yet after five days on the road, she seemed to know the end of the trail when we arrived in Portal. Instead of hiding, she began to explore the new world of mesquite and cacti. After six months we returned to Florida to sell Treetops and close out our affairs. Cat stayed on the Boss Ranch, a loner there despite goats, cows, dogs, and other cats. She greeted us with a restrained "Meow" when we came back for her some four months later, and resumed our old relationship without hesitation or constraint.

Complications developed when one day I heard loud cat sounds from the mesquite. Plaintive, pleading sounds. It was several days before I glimpsed the source: a large and shiny black cat. More days passed before the animal decided I'd been softened by his singing and came forth unexpectedly to rub himself against my boots. Lean and muscular, he looked capable of taking care of himself in the wilderness, but he obviously wanted a home. I fed him, stroked his sleek dark hair, and refused to let him into the house.

Had it been possible, I would have kept Black Bastard as an outside cat, but both he and Old Cat had different ideas. She refused to come outside and he tried to jump inside every time the door opened. There seemed no way they could co-exist. Reluctantly, I decided Old Cat had seniority. She had been around too long and deserved peace in her golden years.

One day when going to the sanitary landfill below Rodeo in New Mexico, I put the black one in the trunk of the car with the garbage. The dump, I figured, would always supply food and perhaps he would make friends with a dumpster. Yet when I arrived, the garbage bag was still in the trunk, but the cat was not. How he got out I yet don't know, but he greeted me with every sign of affection on my arrival home.

Again and again I tried to haul Black Bastard away, but always he returned. And Old Cat, meanwhile, grew sickly and depressed. She missed her outdoor walks with me and, or so I surmised, probably worried that I had rejected her.

Abruptly, the problem solved itself. The black cat vanished. I was both glad and sorry, but Old Cat was obviously delighted. She came outside and rolled lazily in the sand. More than a year later I found some bones and a large hunk of black fur in a little clearing surrounded by mesquite. It seemed obvious that a pack of coyotes had caught him there, a hundred yards from the house, and, despite his survivor skills, he had been unable to cope. Over-confidence, male pride, the pleasure of the hunt. Call it what you will, but it had betrayed him.

Life settled into a routine once more. During winter months when nights were cold, Old Cat spent most of her time indoors, sleeping in a large round basket we bought for her in Old Mexico. Her familiar purr gradually got louder until you had to say she snored. She grew fat, but lost some of it when summer came. In the heat of the day she remained inside, but at dark she wanted out. She slept on the deck, safely above danger even when the roving coyotes came into the yard in search of food.

As her nineteenth birthday approaches, she seems indestructible, at peace with herself and her world. She still accompanies me on slow walks, and when she decides we've gone far enough she sits down and meows loudly. When I dig in the garden, she explores the upturned earth and nibbles on green weeds. Exercise is always followed by a snack and a snooze.

In contrast, my wife and I visit doctors regularly and often, and I brood on the meaning of it all. Sometimes, I think Old Cat will outlive both of us. I hope she does for in her own personal, dignified way, she has made a contribution to my life—you might call it companionship.

My daughter, meanwhile, is back east making a life of her own.

Dreams

Pride comes easily when you carve a homestead out of a virgin wilderness, but it ebbs a bit when you discover that the wilderness has known man before.

And women, of course.

Throughout this southeastern corner of Arizona, in even the most lonely dell, there is evidence of prior occupation, of dreams long dead. Since little rots in a low-humidity desert, one finds pieces of furniture, hunks of iron, and rolls of barbed wire in the most unlikely places. Adobe walls still brave the winds, and blue medicine bottles and broken china lie in the sand under mesquite bushes.

My Contractor took time off from building my house to search for a long abandoned pear orchard up remote Jhus Canyon. Somehow, he and his sons got his pickup to it and they returned with a load of fruit. The pears were small and strangely shaped, but they were edible and would, said the Contractor, make good preserves.

I wondered who had planted the pear trees. Had he or she assumed their grandchildren would enjoy the fruit? Would the trees have been planted if the homesteader had known that bears would come for the pears year after year, the sequence interrupted only once by a man not destined to return a second time? Not likely.

Who would eat the pears in my orchard?

That's the type of question to temper pride. Sometime back, a half century, perhaps, a family lived up the slope from me in a grassy little valley fed by an underground stream. Their household water, however, came from the source of the underground stream, a natural spring high on the side of Portal Peak. Somehow, those pioneers hauled cement up the mountain and by adroit use of rocks-in-place created an open-air holding tank. Cast-iron pipe and gravity did the rest and the homestead had the advantage of water under pressure in cabin and corral. The little pool, some six feet deep, still stands there on the mountainside, used only by wild animals. It's too far for humans to climb for a swim on a hot day. Of the homestead, only part of the corral and the concrete floor of a small room remain.

Inquiry revealed that in the days before well drilling became practical—well digging was never practical—it was common practice to pipe water from high off the nearest mountain. Sometimes the pipes ran for miles. Maintenance surely was a continuing problem.

This type of pioneer dates to the birth of the century when "squatters" challenged the guns of the San Simon Cattle and Canal Company which had considered the valley its own and had grazed thousands of head of cattle upon it. But before the cowboy there was the prospector. Drawn by the richness of the silver strike at Tombstone, the hopeful dug test holes all over the area. Many were deeply dug and their tailings can be seen on the slopes of the mountains all about, but the greatest area of concentration was between Portal and Paradise in what is now the Coronado National Forest.

The holes, some with vertical ladders still in place, represent dreams defeated. Hope remains very much alive, however, and is represented by "staked" mining claims.

The stakes are either driven into the ground or supported in place by rock piles. Rattlesnakes sometimes find shelter in those rock piles, so approach them carefully. Nailed to the stakes is a container, often a tobacco can, and in the can is official notice that John Doe claims the mineral wealth within a described area. Allegedly, many people are waiting for the price of silver to skyrocket as did gold a few years back.

Not everyone is waiting for higher prices, however, as I discovered one warm Christmas Day when I decided to add to my collection of crystal. On the top of a high foothill that separates the valley from Silver Peak, calcite lies exposed. To get there one can ascend a long abandoned mining road that climbs the small mountain in a semicircle. Along the way are old shafts, dug deep and straight down into the multicolored earth. In the past, I had driven part of the distance before being halted by a washed out ravine, so I parked in my usual place and proceeded on foot.

To my astonishment, I found that the washout had been repaired, and there were truck tracks across it and up the old trail. I wasn't tempted to try to drive, however, for I knew there was no place to turn around. So on I hiked, and soon I could see a truck—facing me—at the end of the road. The driver, I discovered, had backed his vehicle in there. The guy, if nothing else, had guts.

There was no one at the truck when I reached it, and no one in the mineshaft, so I continued through the rocks and catclaw to the top of the ridge and thence to a bald spot where calcite crystals glittered in the sunlight. There were all sizes and shapes, the pretty ones worth twenty-five dollars in a souvenir shop, so I filled a backpack, took a long drink from my canteen, and turned back the way I had come. Soon I could see the truck below, and two figures moving out of the underbrush to stand beside it. A dog began to bark, a large dog that turned out to be half-coyote. As I approached, the man yelled an order and the dog subsided.

A man and woman awaited me, each dressed in jeans, denim shirts, and boots. On their heads were wide brimmed straw hats and around their waists revolvers were strapped. Despite dirt and a lot of hair, the man was articulate enough when he discovered I was a harmless rockhound of sorts. He explained that they went armed because local ranchers who had the land leased for cattle objected to them camping at a waterhole down below. A prospector had the right to camp where he pleased on federal land, he said, but the ranchers had no respect for the law.

I knew it was considered bad taste to ask a rancher how many mother cows he runs, so I hesitated before asking the prospector if he was finding any silver in the old mine. He wasn't bashful, however.

"Plenty," he said, and his woman nodded agreement. In fact, he had found a vein of silver running from this mine shaft to another about a hundred yards above. As soon as the holidays were over, he planned to bring in a bulldozer and start harvesting the buried wealth.

I wondered aloud why the old mines had been abandoned, and he shared my bewilderment. There was plenty of gold as well as silver in the area. Last summer the two of them had panned 380 ounces of golddust from Turkey Creek above Paradise. He had the dust down below in his camper which, he added without smiling, was another reason they carried guns.

Unsure as to the price of gold but knowing it to be in excess of $300 an ounce, I figured that if the guy was truthful he must have around $100,000 down at his camper. So why was he up here looking for more?

The woman, rather short and stoutish, had little to say, but the man kept talking, throwing in technical terms to prove his expertise. When I moved away, he called to assure me the coffeepot at camp was always hot so I should drop in at any time. Western hospitality, no doubt. Driving home, the camper was visible in a grove of cottonwoods. When, a month or two later, I rode back over the hills, the camp was gone. Just a few beer cans marked the spot. And there was no activity up the mining trail. No truck, no bulldozer. The fortune-hunters had vanished.

Vanished also are the Apaches who were here before the Anglo, before the Spaniard. About the only evidence of their passing are "metates," hollowed-out slabs of stone in which the women ground mesquite beans and a wide variety of seeds. A rancher in Portal has made a fence of them around his home and I was delighted to find a broken one in the sand below my house site.

There is also evidence of the Anasazi, that mysterious people known to the Apache as "the Ancient Ones." Around 1000 A.D., they constructed 500 miles of canals where Phoenix now stands. Down here in the southeast, a river since gone underground supplied their wants. A village stood on the lower slopes of the mountain, and on an out-cropping of black rock the women met to talk and grind their meal. In so doing, they left holes in the rock, holes from three to sixteen inches in depth and as cylindrical as if drilled by a machine.

How many centuries of grinding rock against rock were necessary to create such holes. And having made them, why were they abandoned? The mystery remains to intrigue and comfort the thoughtful.

For somehow, as one grows older and begins to come to terms with life, it is comforting to know that others have lived and dreamed and gone their way even as you must do. Perspective.

Ants

A<small>NTS</small>, said the poet, find kingdoms in a foot of ground, so why shouldn't forty acres suffice for my wife?

It doesn't.

Nor does Home in the Valley or at the Mouth of the Canyon suffice for the other women of Portal. With children long gone, with husbands freed of fixed schedules, the female can be as irresponsible as she desires.

And does she desire? Each day brings a meeting of one Group or another. They convene to sew, to paint, to talk learnedly of Charles Dickens, to learn and practice Spanish. The agile go on hikes, and on jaunts to distant ghost towns, quaint old inns, art shows and bazaars. They do good works and seemingly never get tired of seeing each other day after day. Certainly, they never run out of anything to talk about.

Meanwhile, back at the ranch, their husbands find amusement as best they can.

Fighting ants, for instance.

Let me quickly reassure the prospective pioneer that ants of Arizona cannot compare in ferocity with the fire ants of Florida. The latter can put you in the hospital very quickly. I know; one day while wearing Wellington boots, I stepped on a nest of fire ants. In the time required to unhitch a trailer, I was bitten scores of times and within minutes could hardly stand. Ankles and feet were a mass of sores and so swollen I could scarcely get the boots off. The pain was, indeed, like fire. Medical attention was necessary.

No, the Harvester Ant of Arizona is placid enough on the ground, but watch out when he grows wings. We learned the hard way. Coming back from somewhere in mid-afternoon, we opened the door and found the main room occupied by thousands, perhaps millions, of flying ants. They had spread over the tile floor and were exploring the walls and ceiling, searching for I know not what. Faye grabbed a can of insect spray while I raced to the fireplace and closed the glass doors. The damned ants were coming down the chimney. I ran out the door and up to the deck. The top of the chimney was covered with ants waiting their turn to descend and millions more flew around it waiting a chance to land. I found a wide board, got the ladder and some bricks, and sealed the top of the chimney. Ants swarmed all over me in the process. Had they been Florida fire ants I might never have reached the ground. Even so, they plugged my nostrils and filled my mouth when I opened it for air.

It took us a week to clean them out of the house. Where the rest of the swarm went, I never noticed. Thereafter, as quickly as the ashes of the last fire of winter cooled, I closed off the chimney.

Months passed and the episode was superseded by others as we adjusted to the old frontier. Then, one day, I found a colony of red ants just outside my garden gate. Since it was an area I'd be frequently using, and remembering the Florida incident, I decided to persuade the little devils to go hence. I turned the garden hose upon the two little holes they use to exit and enter, washing away several inches of top soil and certainly flooding the kingdom below. It looked like a disaster area worthy of federal aid when I stopped, but next day everything seemed back to normal. The ants came and went, ranging afar in all directions, busy, always busy.

Well, I decided, they really weren't harming anything and one had to admire their persistence in the face of what must have seemed to be unusual adversity. Live and let live and all that non-violent stuff.

Summer came and I went often to the garden, trying to persuade corn and beans and tomatoes to grow among the rocks that had escaped me when I dug the place up. When one day I noticed that many of the ants outside my gate had developed wings, I became alarmed. Local antwatchers told me the winged ones were capable of reproduction and were intended to form new kingdoms. Remembering their invasion of my house, I determined they would not reproduce in numbers in my back yard.

With pick and shovel, I assaulted their underground empire. Their tunnels, I found, ran parallel to the surface and were full of white eggs. Brutally I shovelled up dirt and eggs, scattering them in all directions. Holes remained, so I dug down a couple of feet until the place began to resemble an excavation for a swimming pool. What ants remained ran hither and thither seeking, no doubt, to ascertain what angry god had laid waste their kingdom and what to do to appease him. Well satisfied, I went on to other labors.

Next morning, the ants had regrouped and were in their usual routine, coming and going. I borrowed my wife's insect spray and began chemical warfare. Nothing moved when at last I stopped.

No. The ants either revived or reinforcements from deep within the earth came up. When I checked next day they were hard at work once more. In disgust, I urinated at length upon them, concentrating my fire upon the two holes they used to exit and enter.

It was noon the following day before I started once more for the garden. I didn't get there; a river of ants blocked my way to the gate.

The river began at the long-beseiged ant holes and moved past the garden gate some thirty feet to the vicinity of a mesquite bush. There, at the end of the stream, a squadron of engineer ants had dug the usual two holes and were obviously at work upon the tunnels below. About four feet wide was the river. In the center a line of ants carried white eggs from the old homeplace to the new. A second line scurried back to get new loads. On each side of these workers were lines of soldiers, thousands of them in equally spaced columns, moving back and forth, protecting the civilians and the precious eggs in the center.

It was an amazing sight, suggestive as it was of a central intelligence and an iron discipline. The new site was out of my way, convenient to the garden, yet isolated enough to be safe. Who had selected it? Who had given the order to relocate? And who had arranged the maneuver?

By day's end the resettlement was complete. The digging continued, of course, as the empire below was expanded. A few ants, three or four, wandered about the old homestead as if bewildered. Why had they been left behind, I wondered?

I described the incident to a retired biology professor who has devoted much of his life to a study of ants. He had heard of such sudden migrations, he said, but had never witnessed one. Apparently my urine had annoyed the queen. Only she had the power to order her subjects to seek new worlds when the old one became untenable.

In winter, ants delve deep into the earth and hibernate, but the women of Portal continue their ceaseless search. They don't have a queen, you see. Perhaps they are looking for one.

Rats

J. Edgar Hoover in one of his famous marginal notes called me a "rat" once, and that was *before* I wrote a book about him. The late F.B.I. director had a limited vocabulary, however, and I don't think he knew much more about rodents than he did about organized crime.

Arizona has two kinds of rats that can cause unwary newcomers problems. The packrat isn't unique except for his size, but the kangaroo rat, on the other hand, is a bit different.

During the long summer our house was under construction, I became acquainted with the packrat. We lived for a few weeks in a trailer. Each night we put Old Cat outside the door with a plastic bowl of food and another of milk. Each morning I found a hungry cat waiting at the door with her empty bowls sitting some twenty feet away.

Upon deciding this was a wee bit unusual, I poised myself by the door one evening. When I heard a slight noise outside, I flipped the light switch and opened the door. There, caught in the act, was a large rat. He, or she, had the bowl of food in its mouth and was carrying it carefully to a spot under the trailer. Old Cat was crouched nearby, apparently too astonished to act. The rat dropped the bowl and ran but later, after the light was out, I heard it return.

Weeks later, after I began feeding Old Cat in the trailer, I found her munching happily on a large rat. Revenge was apparently sweet.

My next encounter with a packrat came one cold winter day when the car motor refused to start or even turn over. When I opened the hood a large rat leaped out. Not only had the intruder built a nest of sticks, stones, and feathers, he had gnawed the insulation off the ignition wires and, in the process, cut two of the wires. I found it necessary to wrap electrical tape around all the engine wires in both car and truck.

It's cold weather that drives the rats into the nooks and crannies of vehicles. But they're not alone in that. Once I found a wild cat under the truck hood, but he had not tried to improve on conditions by building a nest. A pity, I thought, that the cat and rat didn't choose the same night to seek refuge in the GMC.

When rats moved under my newly built storeroom and cut a classic half-circle opening, I bought the biggest trap I could find in Douglas and baited it with cheese. No action. Finally I put a slice of ripe cantaloupe on the trigger and next morning had myself a rat.

Caught a second one the following night. Apparently in the desert, a juicy bit of fruit is more appealing than dry cheese. Old Cat disposed of the bodies for me.

The kangaroo rat gets its name from its powerful hind legs. Its body is smaller than the packrat, about three to four inches, but it has a long tail with a tuft of hair at the very end. Home is often under a mesquite bush which collects debris useful to the rat in building a mound about two feet high and from eight to fifteen feet in diameter. It is here the rodent employs those powerful hind haunches to dig tunnels deep into the mound. There are always several exits, holes about four inches in diameter, so, if danger threatens, the animal has several back doors through which to escape. Scientists have estimated that there are ten pounds of nitrates in each mound, and the tunnels aerate the earth. In any case, kangaroo mounds are a source of good soil for gardens or flower beds. For that matter, the same can be said of dirt under most mesquite bushes whether or not a rat has made a home there.

One wonders why in the old cowboy books and movies, the brave horse of the hero always broke his leg in gopher holes and never in a kangaroo rat's underground complex. In this part of the west, at least, rats outnumber gophers by a wide margin, and a kangaroo's mound is a real booby trap. Even more so, I suppose, if a rattlesnake has moved in to share the premises.

My problems with the species began when I planted my first garden. Nothing came up. I replanted, and finally got some beans to grow. Carefully I watered them each day during the dry spring, and they grew several inches high. Encouraged, I planted some more corn and set out tomato plants. Next morning I was dismayed to discover many of my beans had been snipped, the tops lying close by the stems and looking a bit shriveled.

Looking for clues I found only some triangular holes about an inch deep and an inch wide in my corn row. I sifted through the soil and could find no corn. So once again I began asking questions and eventually suspicion centered on the kangaroo rat. He was small enough, for one thing, to get through the one-inch chicken wire with which I had surrounded the garden. A packrat was too large; I found one with his head hung in the wire, unable to advance and unable to pull back.

Searching the area around the garden, I found several mounds with many exit holes. Carefully, I caved them in. But next day, the few remaining beans had been cut. I located a kangaroo rat expert and discovered that the rodent is an avid seed collector. He can smell the seeds in the ground, it seems, and after eating, he takes the rest to his mound and stores them. As to the bean plants, he had cut them and sucked the stems for moisture. Like many creatures of the desert he doesn't drink—he gets his fluids from his food.

All very well, but how does one protect his garden? The expert, naturally didn't suggest the obvious. On my next safari to distant Douglas I found the feed store and there I bought a can of corn. Each grain appeared normal but was laced with cyanide.

"Don't leave any out where the birds can get it," warned the salesman, a middle-aged man who wore his silver-plated belt buckle under his belly just like cowboys.

Next morning I dug up a fresh bit of earth and planted corn in the usual manner. The kangaroo rat expert had assured me that her favorite creature only operated on dark nights. Like the groundhog in spring, if the rat could see his shadow in the moonlight he would flee back to his home. Nevertheless, in midafternoon, I took a look at the garden to make sure none of the seeds had become uncovered. I found small, triangular holes where the corn had been.

A few feet away near the fence I found the robber. I carried it away and buried it deeply. Let Old Cat catch her own.

The following day I repeated the routine and found another dead rat. Since this species pushes its young out early to build their own mounds, I was confident I had eliminated my enemies. And so it proved; I was never bothered with kangaroo rats again.

No one was able to explain why my rats operated in sunlight, but it didn't really matter. I had a few twinges of conscience about killing innocent creatures who had been there ahead of me, but I told myself the corn and beans had a right to grow too.

I've wondered how J. Edgar Hoover would have rationalized it, but he died several years before. Allegedly, he was reading an advance copy of my book about him when it happened. If so, he got quick revenge. No one wanted to review a book critical of a dead man, so the book seemed almost stillborn. A bit frustrating, but as I told a BBC reporter who called from London for comment, his death was a public service. The F.B.I. is better for his absence.

A Game Of Inches

It was a football game in far away Miami that forced me to think about the most profound frustration men experience as they begin to age. The game almost killed me as I sat comfortably in a recliner, a moderate meal in my belly and a semi-active day behind me.

Many years in Florida made me a Miami Dolphin fan. Especially had I enjoyed the 1972 season for my youngest son was at home attending junior college and he, too, was a Dolphin fan. Nevertheless, he made a token bet against them on every game, reasoning apparently that if his heroes lost he could at least triumph over his old man. That was the year, of course, the Dolphins went undefeated so we had a lot of fun together.

In the years that followed I remained a Dolphin fan, but as players came and went my interest waned. It wasn't until a young quarterback, Dan Marino, appeared that I got interested once more. By then I was in Arizona and the television stations I could get concentrated on western teams such as Denver so it was seldom I could see Marino in action. But when I did get the chance, I was entranced. The kid, for so he seemed, was poetry in motion, and his young receivers, Clayton and Duper, made the impossible seem easy.

The pleasure, I decided, was somewhat similar to the enjoyment one feels when good machinery works as it was designed to do in difficult situations. Marino and Company didn't win every game, but they performed well enough to set all kinds of records and get to the Super Bowl. There, a wheel, or something, came off, and the ultimate prize escaped them but I was able to look ahead to the next season with anticipation.

All kinds of things went wrong before the next season. Marino came to camp late after holding out for more money—which, surely, he deserved—and injuries riddled the defensive line. Duper, the agile wide-receiver, broke a leg and missed many games. Marino, for all his skills, no longer had the magic.

Eventually, however, the Dolphins pulled themselves together and just in time. Duper returned in a "must" game against the Jets, and caught a last minute touchdown pass to win. Within a week or two, the team needed only one more victory to pull into a first-place tie. Unhappily, their next opponent was the Chicago Bears, the reborn "Monsters of the Midway," who were undefeated and who had swamped such teams as the Dallas Cowboys.

The Game was set for Monday night which meant I'd be able to see it. Logic told me that the Dolphins would be routed. No one had even scored against the Bears for any number of games. They had Walter Payton who was setting new rushing records right and left. They even had a 308 pound giant who, when used on offense, had scored on the ground and in the air. Known as "the Refrigerator," he had become an instant folk hero.

No, it looked impossible, but when son Jon called from Florida, we made our old bet. He even gave me the Dolphins and seven points.

I didn't think much about the game that weekend and on Monday I worked around the place all morning and took a long ramble in the afternoon to locate a suitable Christmas tree. My granddaughter would be visiting over the holidays and a nice tree was essential—or so said my wife.

The clock moved toward seven—nine eastern time—so I took my blood pressure medicine, got a diet coke from the refrigerator, turned on the television set and gave thanks that no distant storm on the peaks was blurring the reception. Faye departed to a meeting of the Chiricahua Book Club, and I was alone. Two thousand miles away, however, Jon would be watching.

Just as the commentators began chattering about what Payton and the Refrigerator could be expected to do to help the Bears win their thirteenth straight, I became aware that my heart was beating.

And beating like hell.

Only a few weeks before my blood pressure had soared and, according to the specialist I was forced to consult, almost caused a stroke. But my heart, he said, was sound. Now, it was going crazy.

The Bears got the ball, couldn't move and punted. Marino trotted on to the field and 75,000 half-hysterical, half-drunk fans in the Orange Bowl went wild. A few plays later Marino threw a long pass to veteran Nat Moore and the Dolphins were ahead.

The touchdown didn't make my heart beat faster; it was already going at top speed, faster than I could count. I hurried to the bathroom and took a tranquilizer. Breathing great gulps of air, I came back in time to see the Bears tie the score.

Now the rout was beginning, I told myself, but my heart didn't believe it.

By the half, the Dolphins had scored on every possession and had an amazing lead, but I was losing interest. Repeated doses of tranquilizers, blood pressure medicine, and sleeping pills had failed to calm my raging heart but had depressed the rest of me. Faye returned during the half and checked my blood pressure. It was high, but, for me, not excessively so.

Gradually my heartbeat slowed and I managed to retain sufficient interest to watch the rest of the game. Marino was beautiful; the old magic was back. He did what he was supposed to do and the hopes of the Bears for an undefeated season died that hot and humid night in the Orange Bowl.

I was barely awake.

Next day my doctor in Douglas confessed he had watched the game and loved it. He gave me medicine for my nerves and told me not to get excited. I protested that I had not been overly excited about the game, not on a conscious level anyway.

"But we don't know what was happening on the subconscious level," he replied.

And, abruptly, I had a glimmer of the truth.

That men and women have dreamed of a renewal of their life force, of a return to youth, is well documented in history and literature. One can even argue that belief in an after-life is based on the same dream. But it can't be youth alone that is so desirable. Who would willingly return to the fears and foolishness of adolescence, of young adulthood when, emptyhanded and perhaps emptyheaded as well, one faces a multitude of choices. To have the strength, the good health of the young, coupled with the confidence and wisdom of maturity, is the ideal. "To be young knowing what I now know," is one way to put it.

And what has this to do with my beating heart? What has this to do with football?

Perhaps in my subconscious self I had identified with the young Marino. Not for his youth alone but because of his ability to do what he was put on the field to do—to execute. A man with a sense of failure hanging over from the past cannot help but cherish anyone who in the face of great odds can perform and win. An abstract sense of failure over my inability to improve the world I had brought to Arizona, but only a few nights before I had failed in the most humiliating, personal way a man can fail. Inevitable, of course, but none the less devastating.

In some complex way, apparently, a victory by the Dolphins had become of vital importance to my psyche. Their failure would reinforce my own. Age had forced one more indignity upon me, but if the young men wearing the deep blue of the ancient oceans could do the impossible, perhaps I could evade depression.

Tension, then, had been building for days and got out of control just before the kickoff. Ironically, the drugs I required to slow my heart deprived me of the healthy pleasure I would ordinarily experience in a Dolphin victory, but, at least, I was alive at the end.

A game of inches, they call it.

Progress

CHUCK is a biologist who loves the Chiricahuas and Cave Creek Canyon. Nothing unusual about that, of course, but Chuck is different—he's young and thus has no income as a retired professor to sustain him. So he scrambles, and in an area where professional help is almost totally lacking, he gets by as a sort of house painter, plumber, electrician, custodian of property for absentee owners, and beekeeper. I've used him and found him a willing worker and a great talker which is understandable in a guy whose only constant companion is an intelligent dog.

Things changed for Chuck recently, however, and not everyone in Portal is happy about it. Word spread that Cochise County was going to supply Portal with a sanitary landfill located on state land at the very entrance to the village. Instant outrage, and a public meeting was called to discuss how this monstrous project could be blocked.

For years local citizens had been burying their garbage in their gardens and dropping off their trash at a landfill in New Mexico as they drove south to Douglas to shop. Very convenient, and the New Mexicans didn't mind.

On a March evening, the citizens filled the one-room library which earlier in its existence had served as a one-room school. Folding metal chairs had been unfolded and were filled and all standing room was soon occupied. Present was a newly elected County Supervisor and the county sanitation superintendent. The Supervisor said that when she ran for office people in Portal complained that the county did nothing for them in return for their tax dollars, so she was surprised at the reaction to this effort on the county's part to eliminate the garbage problem.

Various individuals interrupted to say there was no garbage problem. Everyone was happy with the status quo. The audience applauded.

Not so, said the Supervisor, an attractive woman and a determined one. It seems that someone over the hill in Paradise had been dumping things and someone else in Paradise had reported it. This officially brought it to the county and the state's attention, and it was officially discovered that the Paradise-Portal area lacked disposal facilities. So something had to be done.

This points up an attitude that isn't unique to Portal in the West. The general feeling is that laws and legal restrictions should be ignored as much as possible. Officials are happy to go along with such thinking since it means less work and less money spent. The attitude, I think, goes back to the days when cattle barons and mining companies had the sheriff in their pocket and used him in their own interests. Some still do, for that matter, but not so obviously as in the past. A tradition of distrust of authority and contempt for anything that tends to interfere with individual action, had been handed down to the present generation. A fifty-five mile speed limit is clearly such interference and a sanitary landfill, in the eyes of Portal, was another.

The Supervisor quickly explained that no landfill as such was planned. All the county wanted to do was park a garbage dumpster on its property and allow citizens to bring their trash to it. At intervals it would be driven away to a distant dump and its contents discreetly buried. What, she asked, was wrong with that?

"Everything," said the assembled citizens. The dumpster would be a blot on the landscape and trash would be spilled and blow all over. What, they countered, was wrong with leaving things as they were?

Patiently the Supervisor explained that it couldn't be left as it was. Official notice had been forced upon the county by the individual who reported the illegal dump so action had to be taken. Everyone turned to glare at Brooks White, the man who bought the site of Galeyville and after much delay finally got a home built there. He hurriedly explained he just wanted the mess in Paradise cleaned up—he had no idea he was setting wheels in motion that would upset his fellow citizens.

I took advantage of the pause to ask what was wrong with burying garbage in the garden. It enriched the soil, didn't it?

The Sanitation Superintendent informed me that it was illegal to bury garbage in one's garden, and he produced a copy of the state law. There, in black and white, the law stated that only ranches of 160 acres or more could apply for a permit to dispose of wastes.

"How do you enforce that?" I asked, and drew only a smile and a shrug from the official.

Indignation increased in the room, however. This was "Big Brother" on an even larger scale. One citizen even suggested it was a communist conspiracy on the part of the state government.

The argument—it ceased to be a debate—continued for another hour. Finally, as much to terminate the meeting as anything else, someone suggested a committee find a more suitable site for the dumpster. The crowd approved, and moved outside to tell each other the site should be far off in the mesquite. The county could put it there but the county couldn't stop individuals from taking their trash to New Mexico as they were now doing. And, for that matter, burying their garbage in their gardens.

Months passed, and people began to hope that the county had conveniently forgotten the matter. A committee did suggest several isolated sites, but no reply came from Bisbee. Just as people began to congratulate themselves and talk proudly of the power of public opinion, the blow fell. A compromise had been reached. A Portal citizen would be appointed sanitation supervisor. He would fix up a truck so trash could be securely hauled and park it twice a week at the original site proposed. Folks could put their trash in large garbage bags and take it to the truck. It would then be hauled to New Mexico and dumped.

For the achievement of such progress, $16,000 had been allotted. Part of it would, alas, have to go to New Mexico since that state had been forced to recognize that Arizonians were using its facilities. The rest would be the salary of the citizen hauling the trash.

.And that's when Chuck got into the act.

The only citizen to apply for the job, he rigged a small trailer with chicken-wire sides and a blue, plastic tarpaulin and parks it each Monday and Thursday at the designated spot. Unhooking it from his pickup, he goes about his business for four hours, then he comes back, hooks it to the truck and drives to New Mexico.

Many indignant citizens boycotted the facility and gave Chuck the cold shoulder. They seemed to feel that he had betrayed the community, and on many days there were only a couple of bags deposited in the trailer. As often as not, they were mine. As far as I am concerned, it is better to drive two miles than twenty.

But I still bury my garbage in the garden.

The Mad Bull

THE COWBOY is a myth still cherished in the West, but barbed wire and windmills made him obsolete. Today's rancher may have one assistant, usually a son or nephew, and fewer mother cows with which to contend. Conditions vary, but in the San Simon Valley it takes 320 acres for each animal, and the "environmentalists" argue the land is being over-grazed.

In the old days around the turn of the century, The San Simon Cattle and Canal Company ran thousands of head and employed dozens of cowboys for "one dollar a day and found." Stockholders in the company were largely British aristocrats who sent their second sons to Arizona to manage their interests. A series of droughts made the business risky, and by 1905 the homesteaders could no longer be driven out. The company sold its cattle to individuals who formed smaller ranches, built fences, and used wind power to pump water.

The valley remained "open range" even when some of the ranchers subdivided their land and began selling off forty-acre hunks. Simply put, it means the ranchers can have their cake and eat it too. Unless the modern homesteader wants to enclose his little kingdom with barbed wire, the cows are still free to roam. Shortly after we moved into our new home we awoke one morning to see a huge black bull standing just outside our wall of glass and gazing inscrutably into our bedroom. What was on his mind? I rushed outside and did what I had to do to move him off.

Cows are fairly easily stampeded. Get one to run and the others will follow, but a bull is a different matter. Throw rocks at him, curse loudly, brandish a stick, and maybe he'll move ten feet, stop, and wait for the show to be repeated. Upon consulting some experts, however, I learned that a shotgun properly handled can move the bull without harming him.

One wonders what the animals find to eat on the mesquite-choked hills and flatlands. Ranchers fence their holdings in such a way as to keep the cows completely off one area until the weeds or other ground cover grows back. The mesquite itself provides bean pods which the animals manage to eat despite the thorns. And grazing rights in the various National Forests are utilized. Even so, ranchers buy a lot of hay.

One bull for every twenty "mother cows" is the rule although more may be needed if the herds are scattered. You might think the male has it made, nothing to do but eat and sleep and service his harem. Not so. The bull is a moody creature and sometimes gets fed up with female companionship. He gets away, up some lonely cove far from man or cow and there he communicates with his soul for days or even weeks. No matter that he may be wanted by some Jersey in distress. He enjoys his solitude.

Late one afternoon I heard a bull bellowing in a far cove that led up Portal Peak. Gradually the noise came closer and became more painful. It was almost dark when I saw movement in the mesquite that matched the plaintive bellow. Thinking the animal might be hurt, I pulled on my boots and went out into the bush to investigate. It was the big black one, the largest bull the Three Triangle Ranch possessed, and he was charging down the hillside to a little meadow at the edge of my property. I followed, wondering what the hell was wrong with the old devil.

At a large kangaroo rat mound, one constructed out in the open, the raging bull stopped and began digging in the soft dirt, digging with rear feet and head. As he lowered his head the dirt flew at the rear, as he raised it great sheets of dirt were lifted. All the while he continued to groan, moan, and bellow as if his heart were broken.

After some fifteen minutes he stopped digging and rumbled like a tank toward a gap in the fence. Somewhere over there was a herd of cattle and he apparently was determined to find it. I watched him vanish into the darkness, still singing his song. Next day I went back to the meadow. The bull, using his head as a shovel, had dug a trench three feet deep in the earth, literally wrecking the home of some unfortunate rat.

When next I saw Guy Miller, the rancher who owned the bull, I asked him about the episode. He wasn't much help. Bulls, he said, are crazy, and no one knows why they go on such binges. Sometimes, he added, they find a fence and knock down a mile of it, the barbed wire lacerating their skin and adding to their frenzy. More and more ranchers are giving up on bulls entirely and relying on artificial insemination to keep their mother cows producing.

Unsatisfied with this explanation, I recalled my days of teaching English to cowboys at what was then Colorado A & M College in Fort Collins. At that time it boasted of its Animal Husbandry Department. In the years since the name has changed to Colorado State University, but I was sure it still had some cattle around. I wrote a letter describing what I had seen and addressed it to "Bull Expert," Colorado State University, Fort Collins, Colorado 80523.

Several weeks passed before Professor Robert E. Taylor replied.

While saying he wasn't sure he qualified as a "Bull Expert," he nevertheless commented:

"The bull's behavior as he bellows and paws dirt is an expression of his masculinity. This behavior is evidently under the influence of the male hormone, testosterone, as the castrated male (steer) seldom expresses a similar behavior."

Dr. Taylor enclosed a brochure on his recent book about cattle, causing me to remember the students who constantly reiterated that "a cow ain't going to complain if I say ain't." Animal Husbandry, I noted, was now the Department of Animal Sciences.

Rancher Roy Boss put it more simply. "Bulls hibernate when hot," he said, "and come out when cool. The one you saw was just challenging the world and calling cows to him. The nature of a bull is to be aggressive."

It was Roy who invited us to witness a modern roundup at his ranch near the southern end of the Chiricahuas. To get to the ranch house you cross several miles of valley floor, go over a couple of hills and up a rocky creek bed. I asked how they got out when their road was a torrent of rushing water and was told in patient tones: "We ride horses."

The mother cows and their calves had been rounded up and segregated in separate corrals. Roy kindled a tiny little fire near the chute and heated his branding iron. Placed upright against the calf's skin it burned a 7. He then turned the iron upside down to make an L, completing the brand. Bob, the son who had decided to carry on the ranching tradition, shoved each calf into the chute, held it in place with a vise of sorts, and—if it was a male—castrated it. Peggy Boss, the pretty mistress of the ranch and formerly a nurse, clipped the ears, injected two shots, and used large shears to cut off the nubbins of horn on the animal's head.

It was an efficient operation, the trio working as a well practiced team. I stationed myself where I could see the eyes of each calf and even when its hide was smoking I could detect no sign of pain.

The mother cows made a terrific racket all the while, standing apart and mooing mournfully. As quickly as the calf was processed, it or she was released into the corral where its mother waited. She gave it a lick or two and started munching grass.

When the work was finished, Peggy took my wife indoors to complete the mid-day meal. Roy gathered up the testicles Bob had removed in the process of converting bulls into steers, and placed them in his hot little fire. When they had roasted enough, he pulled them out and we ate them. "Mountain oysters," they are called, and as an hors d'oeuvre they are delicious. Apparently, however, women aren't encouraged to eat them.

Can't have them pawing the ground, can we?

Mule Deer And Jackass Rabbits

RABBITS AND DEER have several things in common here on the eastern slopes of the Chiricahuas. Jackrabbits have long ears as do mule deer; white-tailed deer have cotton on their rear ends as do bunnies.

And all of them can be pests.

Upon arriving in the valley, I took some delight in observing wild animals at play. The jack is, of course, much larger than the bunny, and his tail is black. There appears to be no fraternization, but they co-exist without friction. In the spring when food is plentiful and there is time for games, two bunnies will square off facing each other. Abruptly one will rush the other who leaps straight up, allowing the aggressor to pass beneath. They do this again and again, and so do the jacks. Is it courtship? Perhaps, but it is also amusing.

Finding food is, of course, the principal preoccupation of rabbits, and the time comes when the new leaves on mesquite bushes become attractive. Here the jack has an advantage: he can stand on his hind legs and literally stretch his body as much as four feet to reach the food. Usually he nibbles off a twig and swallows the whole thing an inch at a time. The cottontail is not without resources, however. I've watched one hop up on a rock and from that vantage point jump up to a limb running parallel to the ground. He walked carefully to where the new leaves waited and began to eat. Once he got greedy and overbalanced, falling to the ground. Soon he was back in the mesquite, however, gobbling up everything he could reach.

A jack's ears are eight inches long. Indeed, pioneers called them "jackass rabbits," but the ears have a vital function in the desert. They are richly veined and only lightly furred. They also rotate, and are used by the jack to radiate body heat. When air temperature equals body temperature, the blood supply to the ears is halted and the rabbit starts looking for shade. His home is only a shallow depression under a mesquite bush, but it permits the underside of his body to expel heat into the cooler earth.

In winter rabbits are seldom seen. Food is scarce and there is no energy to waste in games or in fruitless wanderings. Both jacks and bunnies become gaunt, apparently, in part, living off the fat they stored during warm weather. In the spring, they come out in force. I've gazed out my window and counted eighteen sets of ears poking up through the snakeweed. Makes one think of how it might have been when Apaches were out there, watching and waiting.

In the beginning, as I've noted, I found the rabbits fascinating. But as the voracity of their appetites became apparent, my disenchantment began. One morning a rose bush I had brought from Florida was blooming beautifully by my front door. Next morning it was gone: flowers, leaves, stems, and two jacks with full bellies scurried away as I opened the door. I fenced the garden as a matter of course, using chicken wire, but baby bunnies, I discovered, can squeeze through holes that small. I built an eight foot fence around my orchard to protect the young trees from the deer. It worked; but the bunnies managed to slip through to gnaw at the tender bark. And every flower, every seedling, planted about the yard had to be protected by a circle of chicken wire.

The first time I shot a rabbit—an air rifle did the trick— I felt a little ashamed. After all, I told myself the rabbits had been there first. After killing a few more, I assured my conscience that it was a simple matter of logic: I'd leave them alone if they'd let my growing things live. In death, they helped nourish another growing thing—a Dalmatian I call "Geronimo." Already as big as a young horse, he grew rapidly on a diet of rabbits, and, finally, a connection was made in his brain between the furry animals I shot and others he saw bounding about. Thereafter he had great sport chasing the poor jacks. I doubt if he ever caught one but the sight of the spotted monster bearing down upon them obviously discouraged the rabbits.

The message surely got around for, abruptly, the surviving rabbits went elsewhere.

Entirely another matter are the deer. They came in the spring when the fruit trees sprouted leaves and studied with interest the high fence. Obviously concluding it was impassable, they wandered away, never to return again in such numbers. But singly and in pairs they paid frequent visits, usually in the early morning. If the house is quiet they will come within a few feet of the door, apparently very curious about the strange structure and its appendages. Make a noise however slight, and they flit gracefully away.

I've sat high on Portal Peak and watched a dozen mule deer file out of the bush and into a meadow below. And I've sat in my easy chair with a bad leg elevated and watched through binoculars a long procession wending its way around the shoulder of the mountain. I've seen huge bucks with antlers too large to believe go jumping up ravines.

And I've seen them grazing like cattle in a small meadow up the canyon where an old couple living in a mobile home taught them to eat lettuce from their hands.

The number of deer alive and well in the area is one excuse for the legal hunting season. Ranchers complain that deer compete with cattle for the forage available. So each fall a hunt is authorized. The black powder boys and the archers get the first go, but then it becomes serious.

One day as the hunting season approached I spotted a doe and two fawns a hundred feet from the house. The doe was gaunt, her ribs showed plainly. The fawns kept coming up to their mother to nurse, but were pushed away. The doe was chewing on something it had found on the ground—a bone. Geronimo had collected a number of bones and left them to bleach under a mesquite bush. Coyotes had taken their turn gnawing upon them, and in so doing had scattered them about. But this mother deer was eating them. It required some fifteen minutes before she got all the calcium she wanted. Bored, the fawns trotted away, leaving their mother to follow as she pleased. It was a cheerful sight, especially in view of what was to come.

A few days later it was war. Our private road leads up to the Coronado National Forest, and law requires that access to the forest be open. So we could do nothing as jeeps, pickups, motor homes, and even a Cadillac went roaring by, each filled with armed men in camouflage costumes. That night we could see the glow of their fires, and in early morning we could hear the crack of their rifles.

In my younger days while teaching in Colorado, I hunted deer with the best of them, but my goal had been food, not sport. Venison was a welcome addition to an assistant professor's menu when salaries were $3,300 a year. Moreover, it was you against the deer, and the deer had all the advantages in that country. These guys were playing at hunting, being "macho," enjoying the companionship of their beer-guzzling friends. The jeeps came roaring out at intervals, mostly to obtain new supplies of gusto-giving beverages.

Despite all the shooting, I never saw a dead deer brought out. And one day while on a restricted ramble, I discovered a small herd of deer. Instead of going higher into the mountains, they had come down to the valley, hiding themselves in the catclaw and mesquite while the hunters clambered over the rock cliffs high above them.

Will the day come when I'll shoot deer as eventually I shot rabbits? I don't think so. For one thing, the game warden lives just around the shoulder of the mountain and an out-of-season rifle shot brings him running.

On Bootlegger Saddle

The trail dipped down from the crest just a bit and entered a small meadow at Bootlegger's Saddle. John and I weren't making a lot of noise when suddenly a tall blonde jumped up from the rock upon which she had been sunning herself, and ran madly toward a small camper parked nearby. She didn't have any clothes on and her long hair glinted golden in the sunshine.

"I'll be damned," I said. "It's a naked woman."

John, being a deacon in his church back in New Orleans, said nothing.

Without words we made a wide detour away from the camper to reach the rocks at the very crest of the Chiricahuas. The view down, into, and across the Sulphur Springs Valley is awesome. I pointed my stick at the distant mountains and began to lecture.

"The Dragoons," I said. "The great Apache chief Cochise had his Stronghold there, but it was these mountains he called home. He's buried over there somewhere. They hid his grave. Didn't want some soldier digging it up like they did another great chief, Mangas Coloradas, and boiling his head for a souvenir."

John looked shocked, "You're kidding," he said.

"It's history," I assured him. "The official policy of the government at one point was to exterminate the Apache. It took awhile to make this area safe . . ." I hesitated ". . . for naked white women, but by lies and betrayal they finally succeeded."

My brother-in-law grinned, but it seemed to require an effort. An engineer, he had by hard work risen to an important administrative position with a big oil company. In the process he had become somewhat conservative.

A single white cloud hung in the blue sky above the wide valley which lay brown and green beneath the sun. It was cool up here above 9,000 feet, but down below people would be running their swamp coolers. Here and there one could spot a few clusters of houses, a couple of roads, but by and large the land had changed little since Cochise died in 1874. The county had been named for him as had various streets and mountains when the Anglos belatedly recognized his character in peace and war. He had even been the hero of a television series when my kids were young. Bootlegger's Saddle was a wonderful place to sit and meditate, but I recognized my companion was not the introspective type. Thinking to divert him, I turned toward the camper and called:

"Are you decent?"

"Just a minute," came a clear, sweet voice, and I switched my gaze back to the valley.

"There's a playa down there," I commented. "A dry lake. In the rainy season it becomes a foot or so deep in water and full of life. Fairy-tailed shrimp suddenly appear and there's herons and seagulls and things. Guess they come up from the Gulf of California."

"Shrimp?" A resident of Louisiana for some years, John was fond of shrimp.

"Yeah. They live long enough to mate and lay their eggs

in the mud and then the whole place dries up again until the next rainy season. Seems sort of pointless, I guess, but that's life."

John was an engineer but he was also a Baptist who believed in heaven. Usually I don't try to needle him, but I had seen him walking through a carpet of red and blue flowers without pause or comment. It's all right with me if someone wants to keep his eyes on distant goals, but he ought to notice the beauty he's crushing beneath his feet.

"I'm decent," came the call.

It was obvious John had seen enough of Sulphur Springs Valley regardless of who had once ridden ponies there, so we turned back to the meadow. The girl had pulled on faded blue jeans and a man's sweatshirt, obviously the first things she put her hands on, but she'd taken time to tie up the long hair into a pony tail and apply a touch of lipstick. She sat on a fallen pine, once a forest giant some hundred feet tall, and she smiled as we approached.

"Thanks," she said, "for being so considerate. My husband has gone down to Portal for supplies and I didn't dream there was a man within ten miles."

My companion seemed to relax visibly upon discovering she was a married woman and no wood nymph. He explained that I had brought his sister to Arizona to live and he and Kate, his wife, were considering buying some land nearby as a retirement site. It was beautiful country, surely, but rather remote.

"Not as remote as I thought," said the girl, and John joined in laughter. They talked as I did a little exploring. Tracks led across the meadow and down to an old logging road on the eastern side of the mountain. Not an interstate exactly, but passable to four-wheel drive vehicles. The couple had even pulled a horse trailer to the top of the Chiricahuas; two horses were nibbling at the long grass at the edge of the meadow.

"Nice," I said, upon returning to the tree trunk.

"It's the best camping place in the mountains," she responded. "Thank God, not many people know about it."

I found she lived in Douglas, the city often enveloped in acrid smoke from a large copper smelter located there. It provided employment for many and so was tolerated, but I could understand why a resident would find Bootlegger Saddle appealing. We chatted for another five minutes. I told her how to locate *Treinta* and she promised to stop by sometime and meet my wife. I noticed that her eyes were blue.

In returning to Rustler's Park where we had left our wives and car, we took the old logging road. It provided some wonderful views eastward into New Mexico and downward into the San Simon Valley. John had little to say, but normally he's somewhat taciturn so I thought nothing of it. We paused once to let him encircle a Ponderosa pine with his arms. He's tall and long, but he couldn't reach around the tree by a wide margin.

"Something to remember," he said, and I wondered what he was talking about.

Rustler's Park up ahead was a large meadow where, in the wild days of Galeyville and Tombstone, rustlers drove stolen cattle to graze while their new brands healed. It seemed an almost impossible task, driving cattle up a steep and rocky mountain, but it was history. A road officially dubbed "primitive" made it possible to reach the park by car during summer and early fall, but the place was inaccessible in winter when the peaks were white.

Faye and Kate were waiting by the car when we reached the park. I said nothing. John, after a glance at me, spoke in a most laconic voice:

"You'll never guess what we saw back there."

They didn't, nor did they believe it when he told them. Not at first, anyway.

I'd driven up the mountain, being slightly familiar with the road, but John asked to drive down. He did all right, managing to halt on the very edge of the mountain when upon rounding a 180-degree curve he found white-tailed deer in front of the car. I gazed down and mopped my head. John looked at me with a straight face and commented:

"You have to be prepared for the unexpected out here."

Faye giggled from the rear. "Like naked women," she said.

In the next few days John and Kate looked at a lot of land and tentatively settled on a fifty-acre parcel adjoining our property. A week after they went home, however, John called to say they had changed their minds. They were investing in rental property in New Orleans instead. No retirement to Arizona to be near his sister after all.

"It's wonderful country," he admitted, "but too wild for a city boy like me."

"Hell!" said my wife, hanging up the phone.

"Think it was that naked girl?" I asked. "A thing like that could upset a guy like John."

Faye laughed. "No, it wasn't the girl. He'll never retire. All he knows, and wants, is work."

"The girl would make a better story," I told her.

Barriers

ONE SEPTEMBER DAY I was sitting in my miniature orchard watching the vapor trails of planes pass some five miles high. *Treinta* is on the route between west coast cities and Dallas–Ft. Worth, and there are usually planes coming and going up there in the silence. It was a beautiful day and only at either end of the horizon did the white lines in the sky become fuzzy.

Once upon a time the sight of planes heading for faraway places would've made me restless, but I have enough flights behind me now to be happy on the ground. Happy also, apparently, was a large brown-and-green grasshopper who moved within two feet of me and seemingly went to sleep in the sunshine. After some minutes I noticed someone in a hurry, a small Pinacate Beetle better known as "Stink bug." Totally black, it has a sort of shell on its back, but its chief defense against any and all dangers, real and imagined, is to stand on its head and exude a puff of foul-smelling gas. Presumably, a bird about to swallow him would be discouraged by the odor which may be why there are so many around. They first appear in early spring and hang around until frost. In any case, this one was moving rapidly, detouring around small objects, but keeping a steady course that would inevitably bring it to the grasshopper.

It wasn't exactly a case of an irresistible force about to confront an unmoveable object, but I watched with some interest. The bug came forward, apparently intending to climb the inch-long object in its path, but it didn't need to do so. As the bug touched him, the grasshopper shot two feet into the air, landing some inches from where he had been sleeping. The bug showed no surprise as the barrier to his progress removed itself, but plowed straight ahead. I wondered where it was going and why, but, as I said before, some questions don't need answers. The hopper settled down in his new location and overhead more planes moved people effortlessly across the sky. Like the bug, they were going somewhere for reasons entirely their own. I was content to share the sunlight with the grasshopper, but my mind wanted to think about barriers.

They aren't always physical, you know. Upon graduating from Happy Valley High School at age fifteen, I discovered the other kind of barrier. I wanted to go to college, to do all kinds of wonderful things in the world beyond the encircling blue hills, but a combination of circumstances seemed to make it impossible. It took World War II to free me, and to make college possible. But barriers remained and my efforts to overcome them turned me into an individual at war with society. Such a person is sometimes useful on a newspaper so I made a living, but a press card is no passport to Camelot. Luckily I was able to wrangle a couple of Ford Foundation grants to study organized crime at the very time Attorney General Robert Kennedy took office and launched an effective war against the Mob. Seventeen of my books were published before the fad ran its course, and, before the end, Kennedy was dead and I was emotionally exhausted.

The grasshopper at my feet moved a few inches, leaped, and disappeared through the fence that had encircled the orchard. Speaking of barriers, what had the deer thought when early that spring they found eight feet of wire blocking access to the tender leaves of apple and pear tree? What did they think in October when armed hunters forced them from their usual trails?

Probably didn't bother them very much, I decided. There was always other food, other trails. But what did the Apache think when he first encountered barbed-wire? He believed that the idea of an individual owning land was an outrage. The earth was created by Usen, the all-powerful, and could belong to no man, be his skin red or white. Each tribe had its territory, obtained by force or mutual agreement. No one held title to it. Perhaps this was why the Indian would sometimes "sell" vast areas to the whites in exchange for blankets, beads, and liquor. He probably thought it was the white man who got cheated. Forts he could accept, even towns because they made raiding profitable, but when fences went up the Apache must surely have known that his way of life was ending.

Now I occupied a tiny parcel of his homeland and paid taxes on it.

Something happened to break the mood and I put the subject aside for awhile. My mind returned to it, however, the following spring when it was time to plant my enlarged garden. It had taken great effort to sink the posts in the rocky soil and I'd delayed putting up the wire which not only has to be stretched tightly but buried a foot in the earth. Meanwhile I had been dumping things out there in the hope of enriching the soil. The birds had found that interesting, especially a flock of Gambel's Quail.

The Gambel is a small, plump, chicken-like bird with some black and red to give it color, but its principal distinction is an inch-long black plume curving forward from its crown and usually bobbing as it moves. I first noticed it shortly after we arrived when an obvious youngster flew into our glass wall and fell stunned to the ground. Instantly a larger bird sounded an alarm, a loud "kway-er", over and over. Quail came running from all directions to take shelter under a large, spreading mesquite bush. The leader alone remained in the open, sounding his querulous call, until the fallen bird wobbled to his feet and staggered to the safety of the mesquite bush. The boss, or so I assumed him to be, followed. Fifteen minutes passed before a scout emerged, looked around, and apparently signaled for the rest of them to come out to resume their quest for food.

The quail usually form a forage line about a hundred feet long and move more or less in unison, stopping to peck at anything promising. For several weeks my unfenced garden had been included in their sweep. It was amusing to watch them come by in the late afternoon. You could almost set your watch by their appearance.

The day came, however, when in a burst of energy I arose at daybreak and put up the fence in about six hours. In the heat of the afternoon I rested, and waited.

At the usual time the line of quail began crossing the yard. Scouts were out ahead and they reached the fence first. They pushed against it, moved up and down looking for an opening. A few more arrived and then a tidal wave as a hundred quail or more piled up against sixty feet of chicken wire. The leader flew to the top of a mesquite bush and looked about for danger, but uttered no alarm. The birds finally found the corner, slowly regrouped, and continued their sweep down the slope.

Next day a few came back to see if the fence was still there, presumably. After that they left it out of their plans.

Again I wondered about barriers. One day there had

been no obstacle, next day a fence. Did they wonder about it? Did they ask where it came from and why? Of course not. It was but an incident in their eternal search for food. There were plenty of other places in which to hunt.

Man can learn from nature, but he has interests other than a full belly. Barriers can be a challenge, forcing him to greater effort. Yet some are impassable, causing him to change his goals, accept compromise, and turn him to illusions for solace. Ultimately, if he is stubborn, they can even cause him to seek sanctuary in the desert.

As I did.

Snow

IN ARIZONA they carry the custom of branding things to extreme. Almost every city has a large, whitewashed letter profaning the nearest mountain, and Tucson is no exception. "A" Mountain, as it is called, represents the University, and every football season there is pressure on the student body to apply new whitewash.

One cold December night as Christmas neared, I tuned in to the Tucson version of "Eyewitness News" in time to see a plump young man in a ski outfit standing on top of "A" Mountain. A reporter, he had been sent to the mountain top to give expectant viewers the first live pictures of a snow storm the station's weather prognosticator had been predicting for two days. He pushed up his goggles, glanced slowly about, and announced:

"I can see stars."

Snow comes to the desert several times each year, but, for some reason, it seems to surprise everyone. The media makes a big event of it. In this particular case, there had been snow earlier in Phoenix and that, for reasons of civic pride, I suppose, seemed to make it more imperative that a few flakes fall on the Old Pueblo.

This rather silly effort to record the first snow is, in my

objective opinion, rather typical of what passes for news coverage in Arizona. The general attitude of the media, and, I must add, the public, is that too much knowledge is a dangerous thing. Reminds me of a Florida sheriff who said my stories about his department were part of a communist plot to undermine faith in local law-enforcement. A grand jury indicted him anyway, but such a complaint in Arizona would, I'm afraid, be more effective. Ironically, the most frustrated reporter in the state prior to his murder was my friend, Don Bolles. As nearly as I can figure it, he was killed primarily because he "wanted" to investigate corruption.

Law-enforcement in Cochise County, to get closer to home, has seldom if ever been conducted under the scrutiny of a fearless *and* intelligent press. That, in brief, means the public has known little about what was being done and, equally important, not being done, in a large county contiguous to another state and to a foreign country. In truth, things began badly. The county was formed in 1881, some seven thousand square miles of it. Wyatt Earp, then a Tombstone gambler, wanted the badge. He was a Republican and so was the Territorial Governor, John C. Fremont. The job, however, went to a Democrat, Johnny Behan, and a feud began almost instantly. It grew warmer when Behan's fiancee came to town. Earp, although allegedly married and living with his wife, began to compete for the woman's affection. He won her heart, but that's about all Earp and his brothers achieved in the silver boom town. Lawlessness reached the point where the President of the United States threatened to declare martial law in Cochise County. The Earps, having failed to gain the political control they wanted by peaceful means, tried to intimidate the town by shooting some of their enemies in a battle that has become part of legend as "the Gunfight at the OK Corral." It didn't work, and after some more killings Earp fled Arizona with a murder warrant outstanding. His girl friend joined him; his wife killed herself.

Perhaps it isn't surprising that a people with a short and not too noble history, have turned the facts around and made Earp into a hero. A couple of authors, writing fiction in the guise of fact, helped, and then television picked it up and convinced the entire country that Wyatt Earp and Doc Holliday, his drunken sidekick, were the saviours of Tombstone. The town lives today on the legend, and tourists from all parts of the country come to walk the streets of "the town too tough to die" and go away believing in Truth, Justice, and the American Way. The sheriff who really cleaned up Cochise County, slight, soft-spoken, John Slaughter, is almost forgotten. A true hero was Slaughter. When he told an outlaw to get out of town by sundown, the outlaw either left or died.

There have been other sheriffs since, some good, some not so good. Each has confronted different problems: rustlers, drug smugglers, and blacks. In a county that makes great use of Mexicans who cross the border illegally in search of work, it is the black whom everyone looks down upon. Racial prejudice, I'm sorry to say, is as strong in rural Arizona as it ever was in the South. And not just among ranchers either.

Shortly before we arrived in Portal, a group of blacks belonging to Christ Miracle Healing Center and Church moved from Chicago to an area in south Cochise known as Miracle Valley. Various religious groups, some black, some white, had lived there for more than two decades. Land had been irrigated, crops produced, and a Bible School established. Yet the county government treated the valley as if it were part of Mexico, and many who had come to the promised land moved away. The newcomers were led by a woman, Pastor Thomas, and perhaps that contributed to the tension already existing between the blacks and the Sheriff's Department.

Jimmy Judd, the high sheriff, was a native of Cochise County. A stout, hearty type, he knew what the voters wanted and had worked his way up from janitor. The church's outdoor swimming pool was vandalized. A white man urinated on the porch of the church-owned store. Young whites carrying beer cans attempted to gain admittance to the church while a service was in progress. The county put up "Children at Play" signs near the school, and signs showed children with school sweaters bearing the letter N.

Incidents mushroomed, and after one attempt to arrest a black for traffic violations failed, Sheriff Judd assembled a force of thirty-five deputies armed with shotguns, automatic rifles, and axe handles. The battle began. Church leaders tried to stop it, but were told by a deputy:

"You people wanted a war. Well, you got one."

Two blacks were killed and a number injured before the "war" ended. One deputy was wounded. Six days later Pastor Thomas and all her followers loaded their cars and left for Chicago in two long convoys. Charges were filed, indictments returned, civil suits argued, but one technicality after another conspired to prevent an open hearing in which the facts could become clear. Judd insisted the blacks got what they deserved for resisting his efforts to enforce the law—the same defense Earp used when his gang shot up the Clantons.

The press quoted everyone in sight, asked bland questions, and made no independent effort to ascertain the truth.

Came the 1984 elections and Judd had only token opposition. As the man "who ran the niggers out," he couldn't lose. Only in Portal precinct did the vote go against him, but he got sixteen more votes than Walter Mondale who lost to President Reagan. I wasn't surprised. Just before the Miracle Valley shootout, a rumor swept Portal that the black church planned to buy land up the canyon and relocate there. It caused instant panic before proving to be a sick joke.

Yet who can say the press doesn't cover the things people really want to know about? That TV reporter on "A" Mountain finally got some snowflakes about 1 A.M. and much ado was made of it. The same storm dumped four inches on the high desert around isolated Portal where it got no publicity but was pretty.

And white.

Rain

ACROSS THE VALLEY in New Mexico, highway signs advise that Courtesy Pays. At least they do during the dry season. Come July, however, the triangular signs are unfolded and become diamond-shaped. The message then is not to enter the dip ahead if it has water in it.

Arizona, as usual, is more casual, less specific, content to warn the low spot ahead may be a Flash Flood Area. Despite the warnings, a number of people die each year when caught in a dip or culvert by a wave of unexpected water. I thought it strange that most such deaths occur in the larger cities, Phoenix and Tucson, until I drove west one day along Grant Street in the middle of a moderate rain storm. Every side street was a roaring river and each intersection a churning lake. Only then did I realize that downtown Tucson has no storm drains, no place for surface water to run. Each year they let God knows how many millions of gallons of water go to waste while the American taxpayer pays billions to bring water across the mountains from the Colorado River. It has something to do with rugged individualism, I suppose.

Trouble can also happen in unpaved areas as I learned one afternoon while returning from Douglas with a car full of groceries. It had rained hard in Douglas, but for the last thirty miles the sky had been blue, the blacktop dry, so I took State Line Road without a qualm. It bypasses the village of Rodeo and saves perhaps a couple of miles. Since the state line runs up the middle of the road, neither state has seen fit to pave it. Usually it is in good shape, however, and so it seemed today until I began to spot a few puddles and then a lake into which the road entered to exit a couple of hundred feet ahead. Only then did it dawn on me that it had been raining hard here only minutes before, and the runoff from the west was pouring across the road to meet the runoff from the east.

Faye protested rather strongly, but I told her the water couldn't be very deep. There was no real dip along the road, just a few low places. So in we went and in the middle of it the motor stopped.

There we sat with muddy water all around us and no one else within miles. My wife inquired rather caustically what I intended to do. As a man, it was my task to find a solution. I suggested we simply wait where we were. The water would drain off in an hour or two. That met only indignation. I needed no reminder that her arthritis required little excuse to flare up, so I rolled my trouser legs and opened the door. Muddy water gushed in, bringing a scream from my wife who lifted her feet above the torrent and informed me that I was insane. Instead of replying, I stepped into the cold water, after putting the automatic shift into neutral, waded around to the rear, and began to push. I slipped and shuffled a bit but the car was still on a slight down grade and it began to move. Pushing harder still, I tried to gain a little momentum. All the while Faye was steering with one hand, holding her feet above the water with the other, and yelling that I would have a heart attack. I thought she might be right, but I kept on pushing. Just as I was becoming exhausted I realized we were climbing. Calling on my second strength—the kind developed a half century before while carrying logs off Warrior Mountain—I moved the little car an additional twenty or thirty feet. It was enough. When I opened the door, some of the water gushed out. The motor started and we made it home without incident. Next day Faye was able to laugh about it.

Such sudden storms were not new to me. In that long summer of house-building, I learned firsthand of the frightful ferocity they embody. Having nothing better to do one August day, I proposed to hike from the top of our property around the shoulder of Portal Peak to the Cathedral Rock Lodge where we were staying. The route led up a deep cove between the mountain and a high foothill to a saddle (pass), after which you walked along deer trails if you could find any to the high place where Martin and Kay Muma were trying to get their rammed-earth house built. A driveway led down from that site, crossed Cave Creek, and went on by the Lodge. A two-hour walk, I estimated in my innocence. A year or two later all of Portal Peak was officially designated a "Wilderness Area," and well it deserves the title.

Faye drove me up to where the cove began and then went home to watch my progress across the side of the mountain through binoculars. I walked along slowly, taking time to explore various pits where dreamers of the past had hoped to strike it rich. All were in the National Forest, and I found pieces of old cars, abandoned drill bits, and some huge hunks of mining machinery as unrusted as the day they were hauled there. Looking back down the cove, I noticed a black cloud to the south, but it didn't worry me. It wasn't until I reached the saddle, that I realized the storm was gaining on me.

What to do? To go back would not help; there was no shelter there. Ahead was the rugged, rocky mountainside, cut with deep ravines, and steep. Yet up there was also the end of the trail.

I stepped up the pace, moving as rapidly as the terrain

allowed. Abruptly, the awful shadow of the storm was over me. The wind began to blow against my back, and lightning leaped to the ground ahead with a roar that almost knocked me off my feet. Then came the rain, great sheets of it. Within two minutes, the gullies were full of water. I tried to find deer trails, knowing they would cross the most favorable places, but in the growing darkness it became impossible. I was reduced to sliding down one side and crawling up the other.

Lightning sounded again and again, jagged streaks not on a distant horizon but all around me. The rain came harder and harder. I was soaked, my boots full of water. My hat kept blowing off my head. Desperately I looked for an outcropping of rock under which I could take refuge, but there was no place to hide. Of rocks there were plenty, some as large as houses, but they were round or square. Caves existed higher on the mountain, but I wasn't about to climb Portal Peak in search of them.

Despite my discomfort, my alarm at the loose electricity crashing around me, I noted with amazement that the mountain had become a vertical lake. So much water had fallen, it couldn't run off that steep slope fast enough. I was wading in from two to four inches of water. The ravines were running two feet deep or more. Going down one side I slipped and only a quick grasp at a juniper root kept me from tumbling head first into a deep pool. I was lucky the rock-choked washes were so narrow. Usually I could reach across for tree limbs or other handhold so the force of the water couldn't pull me down. Even so I fell repeatedly. A salty taste in my mouth made me realize I was bleeding somewhere. It proved later to be only a deep scratch across my forehead.

Boom went the lightning. Cold now, and miserable, I struggled on. Through the driving rain I could see the outline of walls. Rammed-earth walls. But I had not maintained my altitude in fighting my way across the shoulder. I'd strike the Muma's road further down. First, however, I had to get through a forest of mesquite. Holding my arms over my eyes, I drove through, oblivious to the pain. And, thank God, there ahead was the narrow winding road leading down to the Lodge where a hot shower would be my first priority.

I had forgotten the creek. There was no bridge, of course, but in some distant dry season the bottom had been paved with concrete. It was nearing flood state—muddy water with white caps. No matter, I couldn't get any wetter. The current was strong, the water reached my thighs, but I got through without falling and soggily made my way to the Lodge where my wife waited. I undressed outside the sliding glass door. Standing there naked, I looked back up the mountain. The rain had stopped, blue sky was appearing; the summer storm had passed on. I was beyond caring. Numb. Entering the room, I went straight to the shower. As steam billowed about me, I began to warm.

When I told some of the locals that I'd been caught out on the exposed shoulder of the mountain during an electric storm, they couldn't believe that even a tenderfoot would be so crazy.

It was an adventure, however, and having survived it I'm glad to have experienced it, but in the future when I see a black cloud following me I'm damned sure we won't meet on a mountain. Nor am I going to drive through water-filled dips when my wife's along. I still have a question, however, and it is:

Why is it necessary to introduce the profit motive to achieve courtesy on New Mexico highways?

Old Things

AGE, of course, is relative, and not merely a state of mind. Having already experienced more years than did my father, grandfather, and great-grandfather, I may have learned something they did not, and that is: One's spirit remains young, but the body and eventually the brain betray it. And then sadness sets in.

The oldest living thing on earth may be a desert shrub known to science as *Larrea Tridentata* and to the rest of us as the creosote bush. A resinous secretion covers its soft green leaves and makes the desert on rainy days smell like creosote. The scent even blows into the streets of Tucson, reminding all the city folk that the ancient desert is out there waiting. According to the academic types, the secretion has no functional use, while ranchers insist it penetrates the earth beneath the bush and prevents other vegetation from taking root and getting a share of available water. If the latter is true, it represents a hostile attitude in the desert where many shrubs and plants begin life under the spreading shelter of a "host" such as a mesquite bush, but perhaps it explains why the creosote lives so long.

The bush's unofficial reputation for longevity was confirmed by science in 1984 when a large, circular specimen was discovered in the Mohave Desert in California. Some enterprising students of nature arranged to have it carbondated and to the wonderment of all, it was found to be 11,700 years old. For a plant that reaches maturity in only thirty-six years, that's a ripe old age. What is it trying to prove?

Exactly where and why the creosote bush puts down roots is a mystery I can't explain. In some areas of the San Simon Valley, the creosote holds sway on the east side and the mesquite on the west. Go north, however, and all is creosote. Go south and you find grassland with neither bush in residence.

Some students maintain that over-grazing by the first ranchers is responsible. The theory holds that when all was grass, fires caused by lightning burned the valley floor at intervals and prevented seedling shrubs from establishing themselves. When the grass was eaten to the roots, there was nothing to burn and, consequently, the shrubs could grow.

An interesting idea, but why would it apply to only that part of the valley around Portal? Moreover, it appears to me that the mesquite is dying. In the short interval, relatively speaking, that I've lived in the valley, I've noticed that a clearing at the bottom of my land is moving steadily up the slope. Something is gnawing the bark off the mesquite bushes from the ground up, and they soon die. Rancher Bob Boss blames porcupines for the deadly dining, but, if so, they eat at night and I've never caught one in the act.

Long thorns that can penetrate the soles of boots and tear clothes to tatters distinguishes the mesquite bush from the creosote. Both plants have long tap roots that reach as deeply as 100 feet into the earth as well as a network of surface roots spreading in all directions. This makes it virtually impossible to transplant them. No one in his right mind would want to transplant a mesquite, but the creosote remains green all year, is thornless, and doesn't get very tall. In my pioneering zeal, I attempted several times to plant creosote bushes around the house to relieve the winter grayness, but with no success. The damned thing just wouldn't live in a place it had not selected. A lesson, there, perhaps for the modern mobile.

The mesquite, on the other hand, is as obstinate as the palmetto bushes in Florida. You can't dig them up nor can you burn the stumps if you cut them. The hardest of wood, they make great fires—especially for broiling meat—but you can ruin a chainsaw chain in a matter of minutes if you try to cut them into firewood. Some of the trunks are as big as trees, but the limbs tend to grow along the ground instead of straight up. One can, if he has long, thick gloves and other protective gear, prune a mesquite and make it into a potential shade tree. A small pruning saw is better than a chainsaw for the purpose, but it takes a lot of work. Only the limbs growing vertically are kept, and they must be pruned at intervals to keep them from sprouting horizontal branches. Since they drop their leaves in winter the mesquite is a good tree to have in front of a south-facing Trombe wall. Some of mine are becoming quite tall—twenty feet or so.

Another native bush that remains green all year is popularly known as Desert Broom or Seepwillow. Oddly enough, it belongs to the sunflower family. Indians chewed the leaves to cure toothache, something I've not yet needed to test. In late autumn the broom flowers with hundreds of tiny blossoms giving it a snowy appearance. While attractive, the flowers cause certain allergic people to sneeze. That's unfortunate since the bush has no deep tap root and is easily transplantable.

A warning is in order. Arizona law protects most native plants, shrubs, cacti, and so forth. Unless the object is growing on your property, you must obtain a permit from the state to move it. The logic behind this restriction escapes me, and its enforcement would seem to be difficult except, perhaps, in the case of such giants as the saguaro. The law is on the books, however, and violation carries a heavy penalty.

One of my favorite plants is the agave. For perhaps a dozen years it sits, looking like yucca or Spanish bayonet and very prickly. Abruptly, a flower stalk starts sprouting in the center of the sharp blades, and it grows as much as a foot a day. When after only a few days, it reaches twenty feet or so, seed pods and flowers appear at the top of the stalk. And then the whole thing, stalk and the base plant, simply dies. Ultimately the wind pushes everything over, and the huge stalks lie like fallen trees.

Apaches loved the agave. They roasted the young stalks in rock-lined pits and found them sweetly delicious. The sap, moreover, was fermented to create an intoxicating beverage called mescal. In Mexico, they still use the sap in the production of tequila.

The yucca also puts up a stalk, but it doesn't compare in size or rapidity of growth with the agave. They make great staffs for hikers, however, being both very light and very strong. Yuccas produce a plume of white flowers in the spring, flowers that seem to glow in the night and are sometimes called "Our Lord's Candles" by the devout. A grove of them is a thing of beauty and a joy to observe.

Perhaps the most famous desert vegetation is the Arizona state flower, the saguaro. Pronounce it sah-wah-ro. It doesn't grow in the Portal area, as yet, and it is not as numerous in the Tucson countryside as once it was. I can remember driving south from Tucson in the Sixties in search of a gangster to interview, and seeing thousands of them. Today, pecan and other nut-bearing trees have replaced them.

The saguaro requires a mere 150 years to reach full size,

which may be 50 feet in height and 12 tons in weight. It may then live another century after that. It puts out arms, bending some at right angles to its body. An immense amount of water is stored by the saguaro which makes it immune to most droughts. The Pima and Papago Indians relied on its fruit when all else failed.

From the moment I bought land in Arizona, I wanted a saguaro and one day outside Douglas I thought I had found one. It was only about twenty feet tall and its one arm had just started to bend, but it was living at an altitude not much lower than my home so perhaps it would survive a transplant. It was standing beside a metal building where each week an elderly gentleman conducted an auction of just about everything he could buy wholesale from liquidators. Surely he would sell a useless plant.

"Sorry, son," he said. "I brought that from my home in Tucson and I'm going to keep it."

I asked why.

He smiled. "I can look at that thing and feel young," he replied.

Skeleton Canyon

THIS CANYON, wrote Gen. Nelson A. Miles in 1897, "was well suited by name and tradition to witness the closing scenes of such an Indian war."

The name was Skeleton Canyon and the tradition was one of smuggling, ambush, and mass murder. It is remembered today, however, as the place where Apache War Chief Geronimo surrendered for the last time on September 4, 1886. It's just down the valley in the Peloncillos from my home. Mexicans originally called it *Cajon Bonita,* or *Pretty Box,* and it was famous for wild turkeys.

For many years Mexican smugglers used the canyon as part of an unofficial trade route that crossed the international border at Guadalupe Pass, moved northward up the Animas Valley, crossed the Peloncillos by way of the canyon into the San Simon Valley, and proceeded westward across the lower reaches of the Chiricahuas through what today is known as Rucker Canyon. They continued westward to Tucson and sometimes San Diego where they exchanged their smuggled silver for merchandise which they then proceeded to smuggle back into Mexico by the same route.

Apaches, raiding deep inside Mexico, also used the trail,

but it was latter day Anglo outlaws who left bones to whiten in Cajon Bonita and thus changed its name.

There is documented evidence that the outlaws of Galeyville, that short-lived mining town to the north of Portal, conducted several ambushes of Mexican smugglers in Skeleton Canyon. Not so well documented is a tale that even today inspires treasure hunters to fruitless search near the site of vanished Galeyville and in the canyon itself.

In brief, Jim Hughes returned from a visit to his Mexican mother with a report that a huge fortune would soon be moving through Skeleton Canyon. Curley Bill, feared leader of the outlaws, was away on a cattle raid, so Hughes recruited two ex-Texans, Zwing Hunt and Billy Grounds. It was August, 1881, and the canyon was heavy with foliage: oak, sycamore, juniper, and mesquite. Nineteen Mexicans were escorting a mule train loaded with forty bars of gold and leather bags containing 90,000 silver dollars. The Mexicans were ambushed as they took their after-lunch siesta, and most of them were killed before they could reach their weapons. A few shots were fired before the survivors broke and ran; Hunt was wounded. Grounds found it necessary to shoot the mules who stampeded. One mule escaped, spilling silver coins all the way into the San Simon Valley where over the years they were occasionally discovered.

Hughes, knowing such a treasure could not be kept secret, hurried back to Galeyville to placate Curley Bill. Grounds and Hunt buried the treasure between two giant oak trees and then went scouting for a wagon and team. They found them in the valley, killed the Mexican driver for security reasons, and drove the wagon back to Skeleton Canyon, dug up the gold and silver, and took it to a new hiding place. Then they made themselves scarce, leaving the bones of men and mules to be gnawed by coyotes and vultures.

Unhappily, Grounds soon got himself shot. Hunt was badly wounded but managed to get home to Texas where, before dying, he left his relatives a map. People have paid good money for copies of that map, but nothing has yet been found.

A little research, however, adds factual details and more mystery. Seven months after the alleged massacre, Grounds and Hunt tried to rob the Tombstone Mining and Melting Company of its payroll, and killed a man in the attempt. Cochise County Sheriff John Behan was off chasing Wyatt Earp and his gang, so Deputy Sheriff Bill Breakenridge went out on the trail. He killed Grounds and brought in a badly wounded Hunt. A brother, Hugh Hunt, showed up, and took the wounded man from the hospital in the middle of the night. A month later, Hugh returned alone. His brother, he said, had been recuperating in the Chiricahuas when Apaches came along and killed him. A posse went out to the grave and dug up a body, but bullet wounds in the face made identification impossible. Sadly, Hugh Hunt went back to Texas.

Cynics have said that the Hunt brothers may have killed a wandering prospector, buried him, and, with the heat off, dug up the treasure at their leisure. One wonders, however, why, if such a fortune was in their possession, Grounds and Hunt would risk their lives to rob the mining company.

History in Cochise County is an incomplete volume, unfortunately, with many pages missing. In any event, the canyon was the scene of many a bloody battle between outlaw and smuggler, between Apache and the U.S. Army. Peace came in 1886 when Geronimo and his tattered followers, a mere handful of men, women, and children, were persuaded by Lt. Charles Gatewood, aided by Apache scouts, to return from deep Mexico to surrender to General Miles. There is no need to tell that sad story; it is well documented in several volumes. The meeting took place on the Arizona side of the canyon, in a wide, meadow-like spot near the entrance. Geronimo was escorted personally by Miles some seventy miles to Fort Bowie at the northern end of the Chiricahuas. When the rest of his followers came up, the group was herded from the fort while the band played *Auld Lang Syne* and the white men laughed. Placed upon a train at Bowie Station, they were sent to Florida, never to see their homeland again.

There is a stone monument on Highway 80, commemorating the surrender, but most people who take the gravel road across the valley to the canyon do so in vague hope of finding treasure. A hike up the winding canyon is a treasure in its own right. There are deep pools of blue water beneath stone overhangs, giant oak trees that surely saw Geronimo, and strange rock formations. A less sinister appearing place could hardly be imagined. On the right, the canyon wall becomes a castle with towers and turrets, looking for all the world as if it had been constructed stone by stone. Cedar trees mingle with yucca and prickly pear, and there are piles of fine sand along the creek bed.

Far up the canyon we found a new pickup truck half-hidden in some bushes. There were large wooden boxes in the bed of the pickup. And high above, at the opening of a cave near the top of the canyon were two men, digging, digging, digging.

The canyon narrowed as we passed a fence bearing a yellow sign indicating we had crossed into New Mexico. And shortly, my two sons and I found a real mystery: the remains of a vacuum cleaner. Who had brought it there and for what purpose? I've never seen anything so completely out of place.

The low pass or saddle beyond which is the Animas Valley was in sight when I spotted something shining on the banks of the creek. Instantly, the tales of gold bars and silver dollars returned to mind. Had I discovered such a souvenir of the past?

I turned from the trail and walked casually to the glittering object. A treasure indeed—an unopened bottle of California Cooler with its gold foil still in place.

On our way out we could see the men still digging at the mouth of the cave. Had they bought one of the famous Hunt maps, I wondered? The sun dropped behind the mountain and another day died in Skeleton Canyon. We went on home with my treasure. Some day, perhaps, I'll drink it.

Fear

We were putting aluminum skirting around a sixty-six foot mobile home, and I was very tired. It had been a long day, but only two sheets remained and we wanted to finish.

I dropped my hammer while preparing to nail the strip Chuck was holding in place. Wearily I reached down, grasped it, and brought my hand up "under" the bottom of the metal. The sharp edge sliced the heel of my right hand like a surgeon's knife. Blood spurted, a great geyser and then a steady stream.

Numbly I stood there watching the red pool form at my feet. Nothing hurt, and I felt no sense of urgency, no need to act. Was shock responsible? No, I was just tired.

Chuck did react. Running into the mobile home, he grabbed a towel, came out and bound it tightly around my hand. Instantly the towel turned red, but did not drip. He went back inside and got on the telephone to call Portal's volunteer medical team.

Walking slowly, I went over to a faucet and turned on the water. Pressure was strong so I washed the blood from the towel and then let the cold water pour into the gaping slash on my hand. A fraction of an inch wider and a vein would have been cut. I rewound the cloth tightly about my hand and stood waiting.

Faye got there first and found a chair for me to sit upon. Barney arrived, and was followed by Bob Chew and Rene Blondeau. They rebandaged my hand and told me I needed stitches. Faye called Dr. Sayers in Douglas and she agreed to wait at her office until I could get there.

We rode in Chuck's battered pickup, setting a speed record. He said later he had been afraid the wound would start bleeding again and I'd die on him. It was a wild ride and seemed a little melodramatic. I sat there with my hand elevated and suddenly I was remembering another desperate drive when I had known real fear.

I had been a reporter on The Courier-Journal in Louisville, and the executive editor had given me the responsibility of covering a revolt by honest citizens against the crime syndicate that had long bossed the vice city of Newport, Kentucky. I couldn't recall what angle sent me on that particular day to the little town across the Ohio from Cincinnati, but my stories had created heat and the gamblers and vice lords became nervous when I appeared on Casino Row.

Whatever my mission, I accomplished it and started back to Louisville about midnight. In those days, the road followed the river closely and at places was within a few feet of the rolling waters. I had covered about one half of the hundred miles and was looking ahead to home, a snack, and a soft bed. I'd write the story next day.

Abruptly I noticed in my rearview mirror a set of headlights far behind me, and, a few moments later, a second pair. Probably some high rollers coming home after an evening of craps at the Beverly Hills, a casino as plush as anything in Las Vegas but, of course, strictly illegal.

The cars gained rapidly. I was hitting sixty which was

fast enough on that narrow, curvy road, but I speeded up. Still they came on, and I discarded any thought that these were innocent suckers going home. There was something remorseless about the way they were catching up with me, something frightening.

Alone in the night we sped along, meeting no cars, seeing no lights in houses along the way. And now the cars were behind me, the headlamps burning into my mirror. Smoothly, effortlessly, one big car swept by me and dropped easily into the space just ahead. Two men were in that car, I noticed, and two men were in the other car that pulled up behind. I was bracketed, caught in the middle.

We roared on for a mile or two before I tried to pass the car ahead. Both automobiles speeded up instantly, maintaining the distances between us. I slowed gradually; so also did they. On we went while I tried to figure out what they were planning. We rounded a sweeping curve and abruptly I thought I knew the score. Up ahead the road almost went into the river and ran parallel to it for one hundred yards. The water was very deep along the banks; in past years several cars had gone over the brink to stay. There had been talk of putting a fence there, but nothing had come of it.

I knew real fear then, and not for the first time or the last, I cursed myself for being a fool.

It took some wild driving when we reached the spot where I was supposed to go into the water, but I got by it and eventually away from my escorts. Hidden on a dark sideroad, I watched them thunder back toward Newport.

More slowly I went home and crawled into bed beside my sleeping wife. I knew, of course, I could not tell her of the incident; it would cause useless worry. And I also realized I couldn't tell my bosses at the paper. Had I done so, they would never have let me return to Newport. The damned town had been the devil's workshop for a century or more; cleaning it up was not worth a reporter's life.

Years later when I told the story while being interviewed by a Washington Post reporter, he didn't believe me. Things like that didn't happen in his world.

The screech of tires brought me out of my reverie and I opened my eyes to find I was in Douglas. Chuck was looking at me anxiously.

"You all right?" he asked. "You were looking mighty pale there for awhile."

The doctor was waiting but after one quick look she let me sit while she cared for a very pregnant Mexican girl. When my time came, she took five stitches and told me I had been lucky.

I agreed.

The slower ride home in the sunset was almost pleasant and this time I had no secrets to conceal, no battles to fight tomorrow. The war was over and I was very tired.

Snakes Indoors

When one encounters a snake in the wilds various options exist: the snake can be ignored; it can be frightened away with rocks; it can be blasted with a shotgun. The latter is heavy and cumbersome so I've taken to wearing a .38 caliber revolver loaded with shotshells when I'm out roaming in rattlesnake season. The revolver once belonged to Mrs. "Trigger Mike" Coppola, but that's incidental.

Well and good, but what happens when you find snakes *inside* your house? My sister insists that once in our youth in Happy Valley I shot a blacksnake in the head with an air pistol, but I find that hard to believe. It had taken up its abode in our couch and she sat down on it.

Snakes do seek warm places when the weather turns abruptly cold as sometimes it does in Arizona. Such happened on September 5. It was one of those days when you wished you'd stayed in bed. As a matter of fact, I returned to the bed in the afternoon to rest my aching legs. Suddenly Faye screamed. I hit the floor running and upon reaching the living room found my wife in a far corner.

"There's a snake in the window," she shouted. "A big one."

And sure enough, lying on the window ledge, soaking

up the feeble sunlight through the Trombe wall was a four-footer. Sort of gray with a long, tapering tail. Not poisonous, I decided, but something on the order of what we called a "racer" back east. Indeed, some brave souls I've read about might well have made a pet of it and carried it about in their shirts.

First I attempted to get him off the ledge to the floor where, with luck, I might guide him to the now open door. Instead of cooperating, he crawled behind a section of concrete wall where he could still enjoy the sun and not be bothered. I got a long stick and pinned him down. With another stick, I ground his head into the concrete ledge. Then I pushed him out and flipped him across the tile. Old Cat, who had been watching with some interest, scurried away as the snake sped past her. Lifting his body on the stick I carried it outside and left it for a roadrunner or a raven. I quit giving "decent burials" a long time ago.

Some small discussion followed about how the snake got inside, and I promised that on the morrow when I felt better I'd make an inspection. Darkness came and after a light supper I went back to the bed. Just as I was beginning to relax, Faye screamed again.

"There's another snake. I think it's a rattler."

That brought me on the double. Faye pointed to the guest bathroom off the study.

"I went in there and just as I sat down this little snake came sliding in under the door. He's cream with black spots like a baby rattler."

It was easy to see how the snake arrived. The front door was open and the storm door was ajar just enough for a boneless snake to enter. And her talk of "baby rattlers" pricked a nerve. Just last week I had chased a large rattler into a kangaroo rat hole and heard the buzzing of little rattles as he arrived. It was that time of year.

Cautiously I approached the open door of the bathroom.

The snake lay there as if perfectly at home. He was perhaps eighteen inches long, and was colored just as Faye had described. I looked at his tail but at that moment he moved. I swung the machete I'd picked up and sparks flew as the metal hit the tile. The little fellow scooted into a four inch space between the lavatory cabinet and the wall. I tried to pin him with a stick, but he found a hole where the drain pipe came out of the cabinet to go through the wall. (The plumbers had been drunk the day they installed it.) Into the hole he went, and completely out of sight.

Opening the cabinet door, I found the space stuffed with towels and rolls of toilet paper. Cautiously, I removed them. If, indeed, there was a baby rattler in there I didn't want to grab him by mistake. From the next room Faye called advice. On second thought it might be a coral snake or maybe a sidewinder. Shouldn't I put my boots on?

That last seemed a good idea. If the snake came out I could stomp him. Faye didn't want to but she consented to watch the door from a distance while I got my boots. Nothing came out in the interval, she reported.

With all the stuff in storage removed, there remained the plywood bottom of the cabinet some two inches above the bathroom floor. Room enough for a snake to find sanctuary and one hell of a quandary for me. There was an inch or so of space where the drain pipe came up through the plywood so I poked a stick down it hoping to scare the critter out. It worked. He stuck abut three inches of his body out in the space between the cabinet and the wall. I swung my machete. Again sparks flew and the snake withdrew into his hidey-hole.

A long wait followed. For fifteen minutes or more I sat on the toilet seat in my pajamas and boots waiting for the snake to emerge. Bored, I found myself thinking about a time in Florida when I stood on a balcony outside a second story apartment. Inside the apartment was a possible witness I had long been seeking, a call girl named Judy. The rain fell in torrents—twenty inches in twenty-four hours—but like the snake, the damned woman wouldn't come out. In the parking lot below, crooked cops waited to see if she did talk, and I got wetter and wetter.

The memory of rain gave me an idea so I poured several glasses of it into the cabinet and down the little hole. Allegedly, rattlers dislike water. Nothing happened except the water eventually leaked out from beneath the cabinet and came creeping across the tile to my boots.

Okay, if water wouldn't work, then maybe fire would. I wadded up a great pile of toilet paper, set it ablaze, threw it into the cabinet and stuffed it down the hole by the drain pipe. There was a curious sizzling sound and a little spiral of black smoke came out. But no snake.

After another long wait, Faye suggested we stuff towels under the bathroom door and go to bed, leaving the problem until tomorrow. I declined, knowing full well I wouldn't sleep for thinking about the damned snake. So, instead, I went out into the night to my tool shed and got my chain saw. If the snake wouldn't come to me, I'd go to it.

The saw hadn't been used for quite some time and I pulled on the cord for ten minutes until my ever-loving wife was warning me I'd have a heart attack. Then it caught. Ever turn on a chain saw inside a house? It makes one helluva racket. The noise alone should've scared any intelligent snake out of its hole.

It didn't, so I applied the end of the saw to the plywood and cut back along the edge of the cabinet. Then I did the same thing on the other side. I couldn't get the saw in position to cut along the front, so I smacked it with a hammer I'd brought along. The piece of wood fell to the floor inside the cabinet. I peered in but saw nothing move.

Still not willing to put my hand too close to a baby rattler, I used ice tongs to lift out the plywood. Darkness there, and nothing more. I got a light and at last could see the tile beneath the cabinet. Nothing.

Hey, wait a minute! There was something. Using the tongs I lifted out a two inch piece of something. And sticking to the side of the cabinet was yet another piece. I got it out. Examination proved it to be a fragment of skin and some cooked white meat beneath.

I remembered the sizzling sound and the black smoke when I put in the burning paper. Apparently the snake had climbed up above the water and had been burned there.

Feeling just a bit foolish, I closed the door on the mess and went to bed. It had taken a machete, a hammer, a chain saw, fire and water, to dispose of an eighteen-inch snake. Overkill.

I cleaned up next day and, being a man of prudence, not only fixed the storm door so it would close tightly but I made myself a snake stick and hung it on the rack with the muzzleloader my grandfather handed down. It has a strong, flexible wire with a loop or noose at one end and a handle with which to jerk hard at the other. So far I've tried it on the cat's tail and it works perfectly.

About a week later I turned over an old board and found another snake exactly like the one in the bathroom. This time I was able to examine closely. Then I went to the Portal Library and found a picture of it. A Sonoran Lyre it is called because of the markings on its head. It is native to this area and . . .

It is perfectly harmless.

Tears

A BREEZE STIRRED and across a gray valley floor the tumbleweeds came bouncing. Others before them had lodged against the fences, forming ramps up which these latecomers rolled. Legend has it that a tumbleweed can ruin a car's radiator so I alternately slowed and speeded to avoid them. My mind, however, went off in a new direction. I found myself thinking of another time and place when I stood with a friend on Casino Row in the Ohio River town of Newport.

The long battle against syndicate gambling and local vice had ended in victory for the reformers. For days, gamblers had packed every plane going south to Miami or west to Las Vegas. Now, on the street they left behind, nothing moved. Not a single car was parked where once two men kept busy feeding the parking meters so suckers could lose their money without distraction. My friend, Special Agent Frank Staab, spoke in wonder:

"Reminds me of a western movie when the gold has played out. Any minute now we'll see a tumbleweed roll down Casino Row."

From whence the tumbleweed would come, my companion didn't say. For him tumbleweeds were just part of the folklore of ghost towns, and some people had long predicted that without gambling Newport would become just that. (It didn't.) Yet as I drove through empty spaces in Arizona, a long time later, I didn't ask where the tumbleweeds I was dodging came from either. They were just something, real or imagined, one took for granted. It was a year later before the question became important.

My little orchard of fruit and nut trees, protected by a tall fence, suddenly developed an enemy within. In digging holes for the trees, and for fence posts, I had disturbed the earth. Weeds grew immediately. I pulled up the snakeweed, dug up the wild-rhubarb with its bitter roots, and stepped on the pods of loco-weeds. A few green things I left thinking they might prove to be wild poppies or some such. Instead, with the coming of the rainy season, they developed into monsters. Larger and larger they became, filling the space between my young trees. Well, it was hot and the trees weren't going to produce for a couple of years or more, so I let the jungle alone. It wasn't until the dry season that I realized what my little green plants had become.

Their color faded: the plants became balls of prickly sticks. Four feet high they were and six feet in circumference, yet each was held and nourished by a single tap root. As the dry season continued, the tap root became brittle. Sooner or later a wind would blow against the mass and snap the roots, shedding its seeds as it rolled along. The winds of March would send it on a last hurrah for by then it would be so brittle it would destroy itself.

Tumbleweeds.

I didn't wait for March. Taking a mattock, I aimed for the tap root. Using a long stick in lieu of a pitchfork, I tossed the huge balls over the fence. Soon I had a pile as large as a house. When night came, I burned it. The heat was intense, the fire made crackly sounds. In seconds all was gone but a handful of ashes.

The following spring I began looking for the young

plant. None appeared until hot weather. Alden Hayes identified them for me. Each plant had its tiny taproot, but the crinkly growth along the stems were miniature limbs that would multiply and remultiply. From two inches high in May, they would grow to full size in the summer, and then dry up to await their life after death.

Is heaven the freedom to go where the wind blows?

When young, said Alden, the tumbleweeds make good cattle feed. As good as alfalfa.

Well, I had no cattle so I got my hoe and cut down the young things. Much easier to do it now than later. It helps, I admitted, to know the country. A lot of blood and sweat went into the winning of the west as people who didn't know the country learned the hard way. If tradition is believed, however, few tears were shed. The cows stampeded, the girl went back east, the Apaches went on the warpath, but the macho men of the west didn't cry.

I learned why the hard way.

The six months spent in Arizona waiting on the house had proved good for my eyes. My Florida ophthalmologist was delighted when I checked in with him. I explained I'd been without TV, newspapers, typewriters. The new glasses he prescribed omitted the prism I'd needed in prior years. Happily, I returned to the west to consummate my dreams. It had taken awhile, but of late I'd found time to begin writing once more and when I did my eyes began to hurt, my vision to blur.

Deciding I needed an expert, I made an appointment in Tucson, almost two hundred roundabout miles away. The specialist said I needed new glasses but he thought I could still do without a prism. I took his prescription to the optical shop he suggested and arranged for them to put the new lens into the old frame. Assured I'd have new vision mailed within two days, I went home. Ten days later, after repeated calls, my new specs arrived. I put them on and everything blurred. I wanted to cry in sheer frustration, but I couldn't do that. Wouldn't be macho, don't you know?

Three days passed before the doctor returned my call. Perhaps I needed a prism after all. Back to Tucson, and this time I stayed until the revised prescription was on my face. Things were still somewhat blurry but the doctor said to try them for two weeks. On the tenth day of trial my eyes became badly infected. I went to Douglas—only sixty miles away—to the doctor who had sewed my hand. She gave me eyedrops so light sensitive I couldn't leave the house until sundown. For more than a week I sat helpless behind shuttered windows, so angry I wanted to cry but couldn't.

When I could see again, I returned to Tucson for the third time and was referred to an even more specialized specialist. He talked at length and gave me another prescription which I carried to the same optician who featured fast service in his TV commercials. A young lady waited on me between receiving calls from her mother. The girl was about to be married and the mother was planning a big wedding.

"I wish we'd gone to Las Vegas," said the girl."

So did I wish she had gone to Vegas when my new glasses arrived. The temples didn't reach my ears. I mailed them back. Eventually, the harried bride-to-be sent me something I could wear—and then my troubles began.

The infection returned. Doctor after doctor prescribed antibiotic drops that left my eyes so light-sensitive I became a prisoner in my house during daylight hours, unable to read, unable to write.

Meanwhile, outside the windows, the tumbleweeds I had cut down in early summer grew back and multiplied. They were everywhere, thousands of them, and I could do nothing about it. It was maddening. The weeds grew larger and larger as the weeks passed until finally one doctor put me on an oral antibiotic. At last I could go outdoors in sunlight and pull up some of the tumbleweeds. Cutting them, obviously, just made them mad. Soon the medicine, however, began tearing my digestive apparatus apart, causing intense pain. I had to discontinue it.

In my hour of despair, I found Dr. Robert Sexton in Silver City. A distinguished ophthalmologist, he had retired from big city practice to find contentment in a small town at the edge of Gila National Forest in New Mexico. He recognized my problem instantly—Dry Eye Syndrome, complicated, he discovered, by a bug that had crept in. Now I knew why cowboys don't cry—they can't.

No cure, he said, unless I moved back to humid Florida.

A helluva choice—Faye's rheumatoid arthritis versus my eyesight—but . . .

If I kept my eyes drenched in artificial tears, said the doctor, and permitted him to dam up my tear ducts—perhaps I could remain in my new home and continue my battle against tumbleweeds.

So I cry a lot.

Moonlight Musings

"What do old men who don't believe in Heaven think about?"

Edward Abbey asked that question in his book, *Desert Solitaire,* and left it unanswered. It gave me something to ponder one moon-filled night when an old and oft-recurring dream sent me out to sit by the fountain and stare across the silver valley.

The dream varies each time but basically I am desperately seeking a publisher for a big story that will *change* things. No one is interested. I wander from newsroom to newsroom, down endless corridors looking for a familiar face. No one knows me and, not knowing me, will not listen to my story. The theme becomes obvious even in the dream: hopelessness, failure.

I sit in the moonlight and smile wryly, remembering the gangster attorney who told me I'd starve to death in the gutter. That fate, at least, I'd escaped. I might break my leg in some lonesome canyon such as the one leading to Cochise's Stronghold, and starve there before being found, but not likely. Sheriff departments in the west maintain rescue teams and have helicopters to pull the lost and injured to safety. In any case, I had escaped the perils of my work and had only the doubts and fears of age to battle. It was then I thought of Abbey and his question. Perhaps I could answer it.

If one rules out heaven and, with it, any thought of a future beyond the grave, then left to think about are the present and the past. Somewhere I once read a statement that a young man should gather memories he'll enjoy living with when old. A young man must have written that. Go through an old photo album and what do you feel? Some small pride, perhaps, but the pride is overwhelmed by sadness. You are looking at people and places that exist no more. You are no longer the person of the picture, and to trigger memories is but to remind yourself that time has passed.

I can remember victories in plenty: the night in Durham when I finally got into print the story about the Duke faculty denying an honorary degree to Vice-President Richard Nixon; the day in Louisville when felony charges against me were dismissed; the night in Newport when the election results came in and a reformer pledged to clean up that sin city was elected; the day I got a Ford Foundation grant to study organized crime in the United States; my first book; and so on and so on.

Perhaps a man who believes in heaven could find joy in such memories, but for me they are but a part of the past. It does no good to look back and recognize how dependent my life was on chance and to speculate how different it might have been had not a certain U.S. senator died suddenly, or an editor developed indigestion at a crucial moment. The fleas come with the dog, said an Atlanta editor, a philosophy I took violent objection to at the time.

I watched the spurting water rise, catch the moonlight for a second, and fall back. It had taken a lot of work to build that fountain and make it waterproof, but it was pleasant to sit beside it on a handmade bench in the sunlight, and equally comfortable in the tail end of night. My wife insisted I liked it because the tinkling noise reminded me of the creek in Happy Valley which flowed by the house where I was born and raised. I disagreed. For me the sound was the present which I had created and it stirred no ghosts.

The present—that was all we had. The past was gone, and historians would write about it as they pleased. The future might be a year or ten years, and after that the lights went out.

I recalled how a few months ago I had been suddenly stricken by a massive pain in my left side and the inside of my left arm. Faye checked my blood pressure and the figures were astronomical. It was night and the doctor was sixty miles away. I took a heavy dose of medicine and lay down in the darkness. Every now and then I twitched my fingers and toes to see if they were still operable. What did I think about as I lay there expecting a stroke? Not of heaven or hell, of past victories, of noble deeds. No, I thought of the little things I wanted to finish: a carport I had begun building; a Bird of Paradise bush I wanted to move; wood for the fireplace I needed to collect; and of a new showerhead I wanted to install in the bathroom.

Would it have been different if I had indeed been dying? I don't think so. Was my attitude merely the realization that I had done my best and could not have done otherwise? Again, no. It was, I think, the knowledge that nothing matters but the little time left and the little tasks one wants to finish. Everything else is beyond one's control so there's no need to bother with it.

To sit in the sunshine and whittle may be as profound a statement as an old man wants to make. For myself, I have, barring a stroke or accident, some years remaining. I can only hope they will be active years for there are many mountains to climb, many deep canyons to explore, and many trees to plant.

I thought of a friend in Portal. At age seventy-six, Mac went to Bolivia with a bird-watching expedition. He came back with sixty-four new names on his list, but unhappy because he skipped a day to rest and thus missed seeing sixteen additional birds. He hopes to go back, but admits his eyesight is failing.

Then there is Bert, also seventy-six, who was with a telephone company for many years. He is happy, he tells me, to watch sunsets and has "no apology to make to God." An avid birder, he enjoys talk, food, and good liquor. Obviously, nothing troubles him—the present is to be enjoyed.

Martin studies insects. He began, he recalls, when as a boy he wondered why the spider climbed the waterspout, and he continued as a scientist. Now in retirement he still studies them in the belief that every bit of knowledge gained will be useful someday to someone.

All are happy men insofar as anyone can tell. Is it because their dreams were limited to the practical, the possible? My goals were open-ended, and not often do I regret it.

The search continues, my personal hunt for a state of being in which I can feel comfortable with myself. Recently I stood at sunset on the rim of the Canyon de Chelly in northeast Arizona. The red rocks at my feet were softly golden in the dying light, but, straight down and far, the floor of the canyon was in shadow. Along a little creek was a sward of green, and to the left of that green strip, nestled under a huge overhang of canyon wall, was a white, multistory structure. It had been constructed of mud and rock a thousand years ago by a now vanished people. To my right on the canyon floor, someone—boy or man I could not tell—on a white horse was driving a dozen sheep toward a round hogan with a corral behind it.

All was silent. I looked upon the scene as if from another planet, and held my breath. Past and present merged and time ceased. A strange and wonderful moment it was. Slowly, the light faded around me and the shadows below became darker and darker until I could see no more. It was then, in some way mysterious, I knew the quest I had embarked upon in youth had validity. I know it still.

I may have dozed a bit. From across the valley a band of coyotes barked and yipped to be answered by others near at hand. I sat erect, realizing the moon had dropped behind Portal Peak. To the east the sky above the Peloncillos was red and I watched the sun lift itself out of the Land of Enchantment. Another day had begun.

Feeling chilled, I went into the house and made coffee.

OCT 0 4 2013